Jan Edge

REVISION PLUS

AQA
GCSE English
& English Language

Revision and Classroom Companion

Contents

Contents

4 Course Overview
5 Functional Skills

Unit 1

6 Understanding Non-fiction Texts
8 Responding to Non-fiction Texts
10 Style Features of Non-fiction Texts
11 Features of Texts – Checklist
14 Identifying Audiences
16 Responding to a Non-fiction Text – Example
17 Exam Terms
18 Different Types of Writing
19 Informative and Instructive Texts
20 Persuasive Texts
22 Persuasive Texts – Presentational Devices
23 Responding to Persuasive Texts
24 Analysing Persuasive Features
25 Analysing Persuasive Features – Example
27 Producing Non-fiction Texts
28 Form and Presentation
29 Audience and Purpose
30 Language and Style
31 Writing for a Particular Audience
32 Writing Persuasive Texts
33 Writing Informative Texts
34 Creating Leaflets
35 Writing Texts to Advise
36 Planning Your Writing
38 Writing Tips

Unit 2

39 Speaking and Listening
40 Standard English
41 Non-standard Variations of English
42 Adapting Language
43 Context
44 Traits of Speech
46 Presenting
47 Discussing and Listening
48 Role Play
49 Speeches
50 Writing and Delivering a Speech

Unit 3

52 Understanding Creative Texts
54 Themes and Ideas
55 Characterisation and Voice
56 Aspects of Genre and Form
58 Responding to Creative Texts – Checklist
60 Applying the Creative Texts Checklist
62 Responding to Characters
63 Media and Moving Images
65 Responding to Texts
66 Types of Creative Texts
70 Creative Non-fiction Texts – Examples
73 Producing Creative Texts
74 Writing a Creative Non-fiction Text
75 Common Errors in Writing
78 Paragraphs
80 Connectives
81 Cohesion and Fluency

Unit 3: English Language Part C

82 Spoken Language Study
83 Social Attitudes to Spoken Language
85 Varieties of Spoken Language
86 Spontaneous Spoken Language
88 Planned Speech
89 Differences in Speech and Writing
90 Transcribing Speech
91 Analysis of Spoken Text – Example
92 Multi-modal Language
93 Everyday Language
94 Spoken Language Study – Example
95 Spoken Language Summary

96 Index

Course Overview

AQA English and English Language GCSEs

This revision and classroom companion covers the AQA English and English Language courses. It will help you with the skills needed for the externally assessed exam and the controlled assignments.

In both the English course and the English Language course, Unit 1 and Unit 2 are the same. Unit 3 differs between the two courses, but parts A and B are very similar and the same skills are tested in each course. The main difference is the extra part C in Unit 3 of the English Language course. (See course outlines alongside.)

The skills that you acquire, and put into practice when you are preparing for your controlled assessment pieces, are also the skills that you will need to demonstrate in the externally assessed exam. The skills for each unit are covered in this book.

Unit 1

In section A you will be given three or four non-fiction texts to read and respond to. The texts will be drawn from a range of non-fiction genres and will have a common theme. Some will be functional texts, like information leaflets; others will be everyday texts like web pages. Some will use presentational devices and images.

In section B, following the theme of the texts that you have read, you will write two pieces of non-fiction that might inform, instruct, entertain or persuade. You will be asked to write for a specific audience and purpose and you must be able to use the right language and style.

Unit 2

You will be assessed on three activities; each one is worth the same marks. You will need to do:
- A presentation.
- A discussion activity to show you can take part and be a good listener.
- A role play, where you take on the role of a character.

Unit 3

In part A of both courses you must produce assignments based on literary texts that you have studied. In part B of both courses, you must produce two assignments that illustrate your own creative writing skills. The assignments do not need to be equal in length.

In part C for English Language, you will do one assignment based around spoken language, or give a presentation on this topic.

English and English Language

Unit 1: Understanding & Producing Non-fiction Texts
External exam worth 40% of total marks

Section A Reading You will have an hour to complete this task. The quality of your reading will be assessed.

Section B Writing You will have an hour to complete two tasks. The quality of your writing will be assessed.

English and English Language

Unit 2: Speaking & Listening
Controlled assessment worth 20% of total marks

English

Unit 3: Understanding & Producing Creative Texts
Controlled assessment worth 40% of total marks

Part A Understanding Creative Texts You will have 3–4 hours to complete one or more tasks from the controlled assessment bank of published titles. The quality of your reading will be assessed.

Part B Producing Creative Texts You will have 3–4 hours to complete two tasks from the bank of published titles. The quality of your writing will be assessed.

OR

English Language

Unit 3: Understanding Spoken & Written Texts, and Writing Creatively
Controlled assessment worth 40% of total marks

Part A Extended Reading You will have 3–4 hours to complete one or more tasks from the controlled assessment bank of published titles. The quality of your reading will be assessed.

Part B Creative Writing You will have 3–4 hours to complete two tasks from the bank of published titles. The quality of your writing will be assessed.

Part C Spoken Language Study You will have 2–3 hours to complete one task from the controlled assessment bank, which may be delivered in written or spoken format.

Functional Skills

Functional Skills

Functional skills are the skills that you need in life to be able to operate well in areas where you need to use your writing, reading and speaking and listening skills.

These skills are needed in order to help you carry out tasks that you might have to do in your life. For example:

- Write a job application.
- Engage in a telephone conversation about a complaint.
- Write a complaint letter to a company.
- Read a holiday brochure to pick the best holiday.
- Read and understand a bus or train timetable.
- Fill in a form on the Internet.
- Respond to adverts so that you are not influenced too easily by a good advert, rather than a good product.
- Fill in a form for a passport, etc.
- Read magazines and newspapers.
- Read and understand instruction manuals.

Throughout your life you will need to use your English skills – they are not just needed to pass exams.

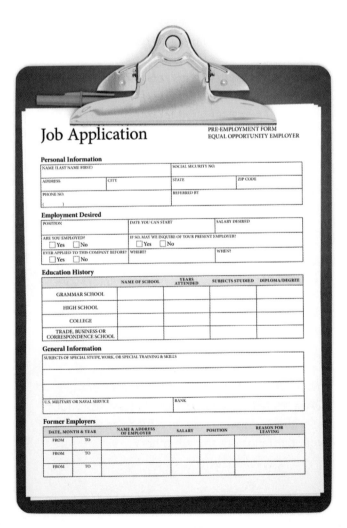

Functional English

Functional English exists as an exam that you can take, which is separate from your English or English Language exam. Functional English is based around the skills that are related to everyday life.

The Functional English Tests

- **Unit 1 Reading: available at Level 1 and Level 2.** Multiple choice responses to a range of non-literary and media texts. You have the choice of on-screen or paper-based tests.
- **Unit 2 Writing: available at Level 1 and Level 2.** Two short writing tasks to inform (Level 1) and inform or persuade (Level 2).
- **Unit 3 Speaking and Listening: internal assessment.** Presentation and discussion (Level 2), or discussion only (Level 1).

A Functional Skills qualification in English at Level 2 will show that you are competent in:

- Writing documents on complex subjects.
- Making effective presentations in a wide range of contexts.
- Reading and succinctly summarising information from different sources.
- Spelling, punctuation and grammar, and that you can use it accurately so that meaning is clear.

A Functional English qualification will be worth half a GCSE and will show any future employers that you are good at these skills – skills that are needed in the world of work or further study.

Functional Skills in GCSE English and English Language

Functional skills are also present in the GCSE English and GCSE English Language courses. So, even if you are not doing Functional English as a separate exam, you will still need to cover these skills in order to pass your GCSE English or English Language examination.

These necessary functional skills are covered throughout this book so, by passing your English or English Language exam, you are demonstrating that you can use functional skills well.

For more information, visit: www.aqa.org.uk/functionalskills

Understanding Non-fiction Texts

Unit 1: Understanding and Producing Non-fiction Texts

Section A – Reading

At Higher Tier you must answer **four compulsory questions** based on **non-fiction texts.** At Foundation Tier you must answer **five compulsory questions** based on **non-fiction texts**.

You will be asked to show that you can:
* Read and understand texts.
* Select material from texts.
* Make comparisons and cross-references between texts.

You need to be able to explain what the writers' ideas and viewpoints are in the texts. For example, is the writer for or against a particular issue or idea? You must write about how the use of language, and features like layout, colour, images and font sizes influence you when you see and read the text.

Each question in the exam will tell you how many marks it is worth in brackets, e.g. (*8 marks*); this will give you an idea of how much you are expected to write. The questions might also give you a bulleted list of points to consider. Make sure you cover all the points listed, as these are what the examiner will be looking for in your answer.

You must answer all the questions, and all the parts to the questions. It is recommended that you spend one hour on this section of the paper.

What is the Examiner Looking For?

The examiner wants to see that you can read and understand non-fiction and media texts. It is important that you present your answers clearly and logically; the examiner must be able to read your handwriting and understand what you are writing. Your responses to reading non-fiction texts must show that you can do the following:
* Read and understand what the text is about on the surface, and also read 'between the lines' for a meaning on a deeper level.
* Understand the writer's ideas and purpose.
* Discuss and develop your interpretations of the texts.
* Make appropriate references to the texts and use quotes from them, or refer to them, where necessary.
* Make a personal response to the text.
* Distinguish between fact and opinion.
* Follow an argument by identifying implications and recognising inconsistencies.
* Compare and contrast the texts, and pick out any similarities or differences.
* Pick out details from the texts effectively, using references and quotations to back up the points that you make.
* Understand and evaluate how linguistic, structural and presentational devices (e.g. text in italics or bold, use of pictures) are used for effect.
* Recognise and understand linguistic features such as irony and sarcasm.
* Consider the effects of the writers' use of language and the way it creates mood, atmosphere, etc.

Helpful Hint

Always read the texts at least twice. Highlight any interesting language features, such as clever word choices, and any interesting use of font, colour, etc.

Preparation Task

Download the example question papers from the AQA website (www.aqa.org.uk) and practise your responses. Try doing this with a friend so that you can point things out to each other.

What are Non-fiction Texts?

A **non-fiction text** is a text that is based on facts and reality, and is not a poem, a play or a story. Non-fiction texts can be written to **inform**, **explain**, **persuade**, **advise**, **argue** or **describe**.

'Non-fiction' covers many different types of texts. They are all around us in the form of leaflets, information sheets, books, junk mail and many more items.

It is impossible to give a complete list of the different types of non-fiction texts because there are so many, but they include **media texts** and things such as:

- Web pages and e-mails.
- Factual booklets.
- Adverts – spoken and written.
- Essays on certain topics.
- Hard-hitting articles in newspapers and magazines that state people's opinions.
- Travel books and brochures.
- Diaries or journals of a real person.
- Reports about real events or incidents.
- Biographies and autobiographies (a biography is a written account of a person's life, written by someone else; an autobiography is a written account of a person's life, written from the viewpoint of that person and usually written by that person).
- An advertisement script for a television advert.
- Newspaper and magazine articles, reports, features, editorials or letters.
- Images and cartoons with captions.
- Pamphlets and leaflets.
- Promotional material / literature.

Non-fiction texts can be **media texts** (i.e. to do with radio, television, magazines, etc.). They sometimes rely heavily on pictures and presentational devices, such as font sizes and colours, to make their points. Media texts may:

- Inform you about something.
- Describe something to you.
- Argue a case.
- Advise you on something.
- Explain something to you.
- Entertain you.
- A combination of these purposes.

Informative texts give you information about a topic, but remember that facts can also be used to **persuade** you. For example, if someone told you that 300 puppies are put to sleep every day in the UK, it would be a fact, but that fact could also be used as part of a campaign to make you think about adopting a puppy from an animal shelter in order to save its life.

Other media texts can try to persuade you to donate money to a charity, buy a product, or agree with a particular point of view. These persuasive texts have **bias** in them, which tries to make the reader think or feel a certain way. For example, newspapers often want you to agree with their opinions.

You need to think about the techniques used in non-fiction texts to persuade you to do something or get you to agree with something. Think about your favourite television advert. Why do you like it? The reasons why you like it will be the clever use of media techniques, or bias. This might be in the form of humour, a clever image, a good-looking person or an amusing character, like the PG Tips monkey.

Preparation Task

Next time some 'junk' mail comes through your letter box, use it as a practice text. Sit down and see how many of the devices listed in the following pages you can find in it.

Responding to Non-fiction Texts

When responding to a non-fiction text, you need to think about:

- **Form (genre) and presentation:** What form does the text take? For example, is it a leaflet or an article? How does the text look on the page – have photos and different fonts and colours been used? Is it set out in columns?
- **Language:** What sort of language (style and tone) is being used? For example, is it formal or informal, simple or technical?
- **Audience:** Who is the intended reader of the text? For example, is it aimed at children, adults, women, or sports enthusiasts? Writers must make sure that they use the appropriate language for their audience.
- **Purpose:** What does the writer want you to think about the topic they have written about? Is the purpose of the text to entertain, persuade, inform or instruct, or is it a combination of these things?

You can remember these points by learning the mnemonic **FLAP**.

When you are responding to non-fiction texts in the exam (and also when you are writing your own pieces in the exam or for controlled assessment), you need to consider these aspects.

Form and Presentation

Form refers to the way in which a text is presented. A text could be in the form of a letter, a book, a leaflet, an article in a newspaper or magazine, a web page, etc.

A text may use a variety of **presentational devices**. It may contain pictures or diagrams, or use large fonts and different colours. Look at the variety of presentational devices used in non-fiction texts that you come across everyday, such as websites, leaflets, magazines and adverts.

Language

Different language techniques are used in different types of writing. For example, a broadsheet newspaper is likely to use formal language and a tabloid newspaper article is more likely to use informal language.

The language that the writer uses is the **style**.

Style

Style is created by:
- The type of words used.
- The way in which words are used.
- The impact of the words on the reader.

There are lots of different styles of language: it can be simple, using uncomplicated words and short sentences; or it can be highly descriptive, using lots of adverbs and adjectives; it can be formal, using Standard English and an impersonal tone; or it can be informal, using slang words and a structure that reflects spoken English.

Tone

Tone refers to the mood, feeling or atmosphere created in a piece of writing. Different texts have different tones. For example, speeches by politicians have a passionate, personal tone to show that the speaker believes in what they are saying, whilst an article in a professional journal would probably have an impersonal, academic tone in order to sound factual and well researched.

The tone of a non-fiction text could be amusing, humorous, sarcastic, critical, factual, passionate, angry, serious, sad, etc.

The **style** and **tone** of language that a writer uses depend on the purpose of the writing and the audience.

The language influences the way the reader feels about characters, ideas and events in a text. In the exam, you need to show the examiner that you understand how the style and tone of writing affect your feelings when you read it (i.e. how they influence your **personal response**).

Audience and Purpose

You need to work out who the text is aimed at (i.e. the audience/intended reader) and what the text is trying to achieve (i.e. its purpose). Ask yourself what each feature of the text tells you about its audience and purpose. For example:
- Does it contain 'masculine' or 'feminine' words (e.g. 'tough', 'blossom')? Is this to target a male or female audience?
- Does it contain descriptions of people, places or emotions? The purpose of this could be to have an emotional impact on the reader, recreate the past, or gain the reader's sympathy.
- Does it contain bias or opinion? The purpose of this could be to persuade the reader to do or think something, or to change or influence the reader's opinion.
- Is it a narrative account (i.e. is it told as a sequence of events, like a story)? The purpose of this could be to engage the reader in the story and the character or issues that it contains.
- Does it use contractions (e.g. 'we'll', 'don't') or full words? Contractions tend to be used in informal texts and full words in more formal texts.

Style Features of Non-fiction Texts

Style Features

The following are some basic style features that you should recognise when responding to a non-fiction text. You will also want to use them in your own writing.

Use of Personal Pronouns (e.g. 'I', 'you')

Use of 'you' is called the direct address pronoun. It adds a personal touch and makes the reader feel involved. It sounds friendly, inviting and even confiding.

Narrative Voice

The narrative voice can be used in first person ('I'), second person ('you'), or third person ('he', 'she', 'it', 'they'). Use of the first person gives the effect of the writer sharing an experience with the reader. This makes it more personal.

Tone and Mood

Tone and mood refer to how the passage is meant to make the reader feel, e.g. reflective, lively, amused or emotional.

Sensational and Emotive Language

Writers use language to be dramatic or to make the reader feel a particular emotion, e.g. sympathy or anger. Charity adverts are a good example of how a writer tries to influence a reader's feelings. They often use language to gain the reader's sympathy (and, therefore, persuade them to donate to the charity). For example:
- **Poor** Scamp was found **starving**, **shivering** and **shaking** in a cardboard box. He is still **small** for his age and needs constant medical attention.

Exaggeration / Hyperbole

Exaggeration or hyperbole is used to give greater emphasis. Writers often use exaggeration, especially when the purpose of the writing is to persuade or amuse. Exaggeration often includes superlatives like 'the best', 'the worst'. Phrases from adverts are a good example of how writers use exaggeration to grab the reader's attention, for example:
- The cheapest prices in town!

Repetition

Sometimes a word, phrase or structure is repeated for emphasis. Repetition is often used in newspaper articles, adverts and promotional leaflets. For example:
- Fact: More people than ever own several credit cards.
  Fact: More people than ever are in debt.

Rhetorical Questions

A rhetorical question is a question that does not need an answer. The answer should be obvious from the text. Rhetorical questions are used for effect and to make the reader think. They are often used in political or persuasive speeches, promotional leaflets, and adverts. For example:
- Thousands of cars are stolen every year. Is this kind of behaviour acceptable in our society?

Alliteration

When words that are positioned close together begin with the same sound, it is called alliteration. Alliteration is used in texts to make certain groups of words stand out or to make something memorable. Alliteration is often used in newspaper headlines. For example:
- **F**lash **F**lood Demolishes **F**armhouse
- **H**ouse Prices **H**it All **T**ime **H**igh

Use of Three

One of the easiest and most useful ways to emphasise a point is by repeating three words or phrases. Politicians often use this technique in speeches to stress an important point. Use of three is often found in media texts such as magazine articles. For example:
- Restructuring the present system would be an **expensive**, **time-consuming**, and **unworkable** nightmare.

Figures of Speech

A figure of speech is an expression which should not be taken literally. For example, 'It's raining cats and dogs' means it is raining heavily, not that animals are falling from the sky!

Helpful Hint

Make sure you know what these terms mean, and that you are able to identify uses of them in non-fiction. You need to explain how these language features affect the reader's responses.

Features of Texts – Checklist

You will have learned many terms to use when discussing or describing texts. The following list provides a reminder of the main techniques and why a writer might use them. You will find these features in both literary and non-literary texts.

The terms are mentioned throughout the guide and will be useful for both the examination and your controlled assignments. So make sure you learn them and can use them appropriately when writing about texts.

Accent: the way a character would sound if they were speaking aloud, e.g. a cockney accent is used by most of the characters in *EastEnders*. Accent can be conveyed through the use of non-standard spelling, e.g. 'ah wunder'd where tha'd bin', to portray a Yorkshire accent. It is used to show where a character is from and to indicate something about their way of life/culture.

Adjectives: describe nouns, e.g. great, harsh, yellow, excruciating, bright. They are used to add more detail to the noun, and to build images in the reader's mind.

Adverbs: describe verbs (the action) and often end with 'ly', e.g. carefully, quietly, quickly. They are used to add more detail to an action.

Alliteration: repetition of a sound at the beginning of words, e.g. 'big balls bounced'. It is used to stress words or phrases to the reader to create a particular effect.

Assonance: rhyme of the internal vowel sound, e.g. 'pull and push', 'cat in the bag'. It is used to slow the reader down and emphasise certain words.

Contrast: a strong difference between two things. It is used often to highlight opposition or impact.

Dialect: the words and grammar that speakers use. Regional dialects differ from the Standard English dialect. Each dialect has its own special words and ways of using grammar. Dialects might be used to show which social group a character belongs to. A writer might give two characters different dialects to show that they are from different social groups, and to show a contrast between the characters.

Exclamations: show anger, shock, horror, surprise and joy, e.g. 'I won!'. They are used to portray emotions.

Humour: it may be a funny story, it may be in the obvious form of jokes, or it may be more subtle, such as sarcasm. It is used to lighten the mood, attract attention or appeal to the reader.

Helpful Hint

It is difficult to be funny in writing unless you are writing a joke! But look out for hidden irony or humour in texts. Think about whether the writer is trying to make the reader laugh. You might not find it funny, but if it is intended to be funny you need to write about it.

'cat in the bag'
(Assonance)

Features of Texts – Checklist

Imagery: the words are so descriptive they allow you to create a picture in your mind. Imagery is used to involve the reader in the moment being described.

Irony and sarcasm: the use of words to imply the opposite of their meaning. They are used to make fun of people or issues. For example, if your friend had chicken pox and you said to him / her, 'Your skin looks nice today', you would be using irony (if you wrote it down) or sarcasm (in speech).

Juxtaposition: the positioning of two words, phrases or ideas next to or near each other. It is used to highlight a contrast between two words, phrases or ideas.

Metaphor: an image created by referring to something as something else, e.g. 'the army of ants was on the rampage'. Here the ants are referred to as an army. Metaphors are used to give additional information to the reader to create an effect or to emphasise a point.

Onomatopoeia: a word that sounds like the thing that it describes, e.g. splash, boom, click. It is used to appeal to the senses of the reader, in this case their hearing.

Personification: making an object / animal sound like a person, giving it human qualities, e.g. 'the fingers of the tree grabbed at my hair as I passed'. It is used to enable the reader to identify with what is being personified and helps to create a specific image.

Puns (also referred to as **play on words** or **word play**): words used in an amusing way to suggest other meanings, e.g. 'She's parking mad!'. They are used to entertain and amuse, and to imply another meaning. Puns are often found in newspaper headlines and shop names.

Questions (interrogatives): show that the writer wants the reader to consider the question, or that they themselves are considering the question. They are used to show a range of things about a character, such as inquisitiveness, upset and confusion.

Received Pronunciation: the accent used by many national newsreaders. You cannot tell which part of the country a Received Pronunciation speaker comes from. This accent is seen as prestigious (impressive) so it is used to indicate individuals or social groups that are well-educated and wealthy.

'the army of ants was on the rampage'
(Metaphor)

Features of Texts – Checklist

Repetition: when words, phrases, sentences or structures are repeated. It is used to stress certain words or key points in the piece of writing.

Rhetorical questions: questions that do not need an answer, e.g. when your teachers ask 'do you think that is funny?' they do not expect you to answer. Such questions do not require an answer; the answer is obvious. They are used to make the reader really think about the question that has been asked.

Rhyme: the use of rhyming words that affect sound patterns. Sound patterns can be regular or irregular. Rhyme is used to adjust the tone of a poem, or to emphasise a point.

Rhythm: the beat of the writing (mainly poems) when read aloud: fast or slow, regular or irregular. The rhythm of the writing can add to its overall effect.

Simile: a comparison of one thing to another that includes the words 'as' or 'like', e.g. 'the man was as cold as ice', 'the pain was like a searing heat passing through her'. Similes are used to give additional information to the reader to create a particular effect or to emphasise a point.

Standard English: the conventional or 'correct' use of words and grammar in the English language (see page 40).

Superlatives: words that express the best or worst of something. They often end in 'est' or have 'most' or 'least' before them, e.g. lowest, nicest, most beautiful, least stylish. They are used for emphasis.

Symbols and symbolism: a symbol is an object that represents an abstract idea, e.g. a dove symbolises peace, red symbolises danger. They are used to create a stronger, more vivid image, or communicate an idea indirectly.

Tone: the overall attitude of the writing, e.g. formal, informal, playful, angry, suspicious, ironic. Different tones are used to allow the emotions of the author, or the character in the text, to be implied.

Helpful Hint

It is not enough to merely identify these features in a piece of writing; you must write about the effect they have on the reader, and use the PEE technique (see page 23).

Identifying Audiences

Look at the following texts. Identify the audience for each one. To be able to do this, you will also need to think about:

- The purpose of the piece of writing.
- The language used in the piece of writing.
- The form and presentation of the piece of writing.

Text 1

BOTOX: A step too far

Teenage girl, aged 15, has Botox 'to stop wrinkles'.

How can you justify a 15-year-old girl being given Botox injections by her own mother?

As staying young and beautiful becomes a 21st-century obsession, we appear to have hit an all time low with teenagers now having Botox injections to stop them getting wrinkles.

Tracy Jarvis of Oregon, Texas, has made national headlines in America by flaunting the fact that she is one of the youngest known recipients of Botox injections. She claims, 'I want to be a model so I can't afford to have any lines on my face.'

Tracy's mother justified her decision to inject by saying, 'I am a qualified nurse and I know what I am doing. She doesn't smoke or drink or do drugs, like many teenagers, so in fact she has less poison in her body than most teenagers I know.'

The revelation has caused outrage. The quest for eternal youth has surely gone too far, when even the young cannot enjoy their youth – for fear of getting old.

Text 2

Samtunling MP3s
the must-have accessory for summer!

Well, you've got to have the latest, haven't you?

The new Samtunling MP3 is the newest on the market and the coolest on the block.

You're not still hanging out with the old version are you? What will your friends say?

Get real. Get with it. Get a Samtunling.

Identifying Audiences

Text 3

Interview: Andy Edge, Sales and Marketing Director for Park Resorts

Andy Edge, Founder of Park Resorts, talks about how he started in business, and how he felt about appearing on his own TV show.

Jan: Hi Andy. So, tell me – how was your first TV appearance on *Undercover Boss*?

Andy: It was weird – totally bizarre – but a really good experience.

Jan: Have people recognised you in the street since your appearance?

Andy: Well, what can I say? Yes, they have! And people have been really nice. It's amazing – they say things like 'Aren't you that bloke who went undercover at the caravan park?'

Jan: Would you do it again?

Andy: Yes, I would, as it was a really good way of seeing firsthand what happens on the park and I got to meet people who I might not otherwise have met.

Jan: You mean like Shaun?

Andy: Well, yes. He was a great bloke. He worked hard and really wanted to make something of his life and I'm glad that we can help him to make that happen.

Jan: Ok, TV aside, what made you go into the big business world?

Andy: I did Business Studies at Leicester Polytechnic, as it was then. I really enjoyed my course and decided that I wanted to go into that field.

Jan: You have been really successful. Any tips for young people out there who might want to follow in your footsteps?

Andy: Just go for it! If you find something that you really like doing, see if you can follow a path that might let you do it as a career. There's nothing better than going to work each day doing something that you enjoy.

Text 4

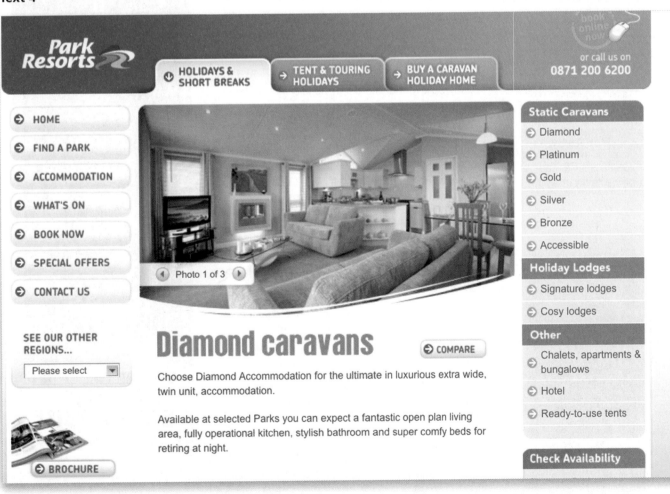

Responding to a Non-fiction Text – Example

Example of a Non-fiction Text

Here is the kind of non-fiction text that you could get in the examination.

But, remember you will get three or four texts to compare and contrast, not just one.

You must be able to recognise the interesting use of language and presentational devices in all of the texts to be able to decide which is the most effective.

This is an example of a web page that you could find on a human rights charity website. You should:

- Read it twice.
- Highlight the images/pictures.
- Highlight the use of different fonts and font sizes.
- Highlight any colour being used to get a reaction from the reader or for a particular effect.
- Highlight any words that you think are being used for effect – to get the reader to react.

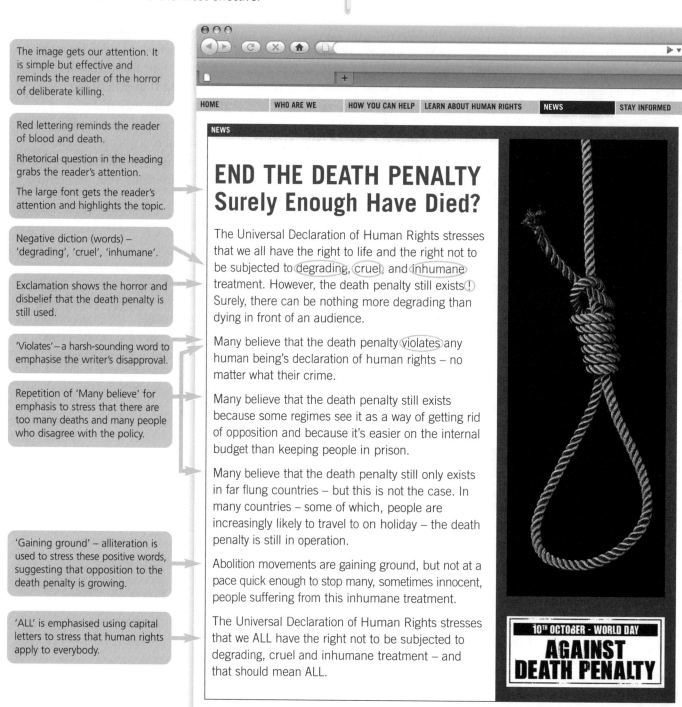

The image gets our attention. It is simple but effective and reminds the reader of the horror of deliberate killing.

Red lettering reminds the reader of blood and death.

Rhetorical question in the heading grabs the reader's attention.

The large font gets the reader's attention and highlights the topic.

Negative diction (words) – 'degrading', 'cruel', 'inhumane'.

Exclamation shows the horror and disbelief that the death penalty is still used.

'Violates' – a harsh-sounding word to emphasise the writer's disapproval.

Repetition of 'Many believe' for emphasis to stress that there are too many deaths and many people who disagree with the policy.

'Gaining ground' – alliteration is used to stress these positive words, suggesting that opposition to the death penalty is growing.

'ALL' is emphasised using capital letters to stress that human rights apply to everybody.

HOME | **WHO ARE WE** | **HOW YOU CAN HELP** | **LEARN ABOUT HUMAN RIGHTS** | **NEWS** | **STAY INFORMED**

NEWS

END THE DEATH PENALTY
Surely Enough Have Died?

The Universal Declaration of Human Rights stresses that we all have the right to life and the right not to be subjected to degrading, cruel, and inhumane treatment. However, the death penalty still exists! Surely, there can be nothing more degrading than dying in front of an audience.

Many believe that the death penalty violates any human being's declaration of human rights – no matter what their crime.

Many believe that the death penalty still exists because some regimes see it as a way of getting rid of opposition and because it's easier on the internal budget than keeping people in prison.

Many believe that the death penalty still only exists in far flung countries – but this is not the case. In many countries – some of which, people are increasingly likely to travel to on holiday – the death penalty is still in operation.

Abolition movements are gaining ground, but not at a pace quick enough to stop many, sometimes innocent, people suffering from this inhumane treatment.

The Universal Declaration of Human Rights stresses that we ALL have the right not to be subjected to degrading, cruel and inhumane treatment – and that should mean ALL.

10TH OCTOBER - WORLD DAY
AGAINST DEATH PENALTY

Exam Terms

Types of Exam Questions

It helps in the exam if you are familiar with the words that the examiners might use in the questions. The following are the kind of things you will be asked.

- **Give reasons from the text why...**
  Here you must find the facts and give reasons. They might not just be in one place – you might have to go through the whole text to find the examples.

  If there are four marks for the question, you should try to give four reasons.

- **According to...**
  This tells you what the text is saying and you will probably be asked if you agree. You will need to give reasons why you agree or disagree, using evidence from the text to support your answer.

- **Choose two examples of language in the text and explain why they are effective.**
  You may have already gone through the texts, highlighting features that stand out. So, you will already have highlighted some effective examples of language. The examiner wants you to use the '123' or 'PEE' technique (Point, Evidence, Explanation) to help you to do this (see page 23). For example:
  P Provide a point, e.g. *The word 'devastated'*.
  E Give evidence, e.g. *It suggests that the mother is extremely upset and beyond grief*.
  E Provide an explanation, e.g. *This word shows what a horrible experience it has been for the family and stresses the effect it has had on the woman*.

- **How do the pictures / images show how you are meant to feel?**
  Here you must look at the pictures and write about the effect that they have on you personally, as well as the effect they are *meant* to have on the reader.

- **How does the writer use language?**
  Here you should look at the words that you have highlighted in the text. The examiner wants you to use the PEE technique.

- **Compare the ways that the texts...**
  Here the examiner wants you to compare the texts. Look at the similarities (i.e. the techniques that are the same) and differences (i.e. the techniques that are different).

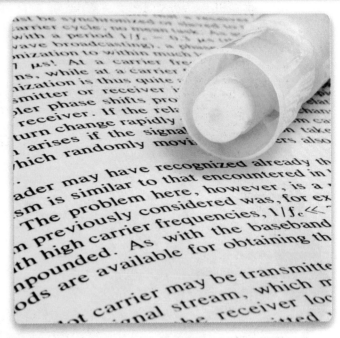

Presentational Devices

When you are asked to comment on presentational devices the examiner wants you to write about the way that the texts look and are set out on the page. The writer will have used certain presentational devices to have a specific effect on the reader. You should comment on:

- Font size and colour.
- Pictures and photos.
- Graphs.
- Use of colour.
- The way that the text and images are set out.
- Contrasts – this could be pictures or font types, etc.

Achieving the Top Grades

To get the higher grades in the exam, you have to show the examiner that you are able to:

- Respond personally to all the texts in the exam.
- Interpret things from the texts and give your opinions.
- Read beneath the surface to find the hidden meaning.
- Recognise and comment on the use of language – the words used and their effect on the reader.
- Comment on the structure of the texts (the way that they are put together).
- Write about presentational devices and their intended impact on the reader.
- Use appropriate quotations.
- Compare the texts and make cross-references (i.e. write about more than one text at a time).

Different Types of Writing

The four main broad classifications of writing and their purposes are:

- To **inform**.
- To **instruct**.
- To **persuade**.
- To **entertain**.

Writing can be broadly fitted into these four categories for revision purposes.

In reality, most texts have a combination of these purposes and each can have a different effect on the reader. Do not assume that once you have identified the primary purpose of a text that you have it covered.

For example, a magazine article about Katie Price and Peter Andre might give you facts about their divorce, so it is **informing** you. But it will also be **entertaining** you as you read it, and it might favour one person over the other so it will be biased, and will therefore be trying to **persuade** you too by influencing your opinion.

The way that an article is written will indicate its purposes, as will the headline accompanying the story and any pictures that are included in the article.

You cannot usually say that a text belongs to just one category of purpose. It will certainly have features of more than one 'type' of writing.

However, for revision purposes, texts can be subdivided into the categories of inform, instruct, persuade and entertain. Just remember that they will overlap and have multiple purposes.

Helpful Hint

Writing to instruct often appears in informative writing. For example, an instruction booklet gives information *and* instructions on how to use something. So the features for writing to inform are also found in writing to instruct.

But remember that writing may be informative without giving instructions, e.g. a leaflet telling you facts about a tourist attraction.

Informative and Instructive Texts

Writing to inform and writing to instruct are types of writing that give you information as the primary purpose. For example, you would not want your MP3 instruction booklet to make you laugh; you want it to inform and instruct you on how to use your MP3.

Typical examples of writing to inform or instruct (as the primary purpose) include:

- Text books.
- Instruction manuals.
- On-line instructions.
- Computer game instructions.
- Fact sheets.
- Wall charts at exhibitions.
- Descriptions of art/exhibits at a museum.
- Advice leaflets.
- Newspaper articles.
- Magazine articles.

Key Features of Writing to Inform and Instruct

The following are some key features of writing to inform and instruct:

- Simple grammar, and verbs that are functional, e.g. 'put', rather than 'place carefully'.
- Technical words (diction) that are specific to a machine, electrical appliance, etc.
- Numbers and bullets points.
- Short paragraphs.
- Diagrams, graphs and illustrations.

Informative writing tends to use simple sentences (i.e. short sentences without additional clauses), e.g. 'Plug into socket', rather than, 'Carefully pick up the plug and gently put it into the prettily coloured socket, whilst you take care'. If this last sentence was in an instruction booklet, you would think the writer was creating a spoof version of a real instruction booklet!

The audience must always be considered in any type of writing – who is the intended reader of the text? For example, if an instruction manual was written for children it would need to be written in simple language, but if it was written for a computer expert, it could contain a lot of technical words.

Example of an Informative Text

The following text is an informative piece.

Hepwood

Hepwood, a rural village, lies 14 miles east of Lapton, an old industrial town that once housed many cotton mills.

Hepwood is reputed to be one of England's 'Plague Villages', a village where the inhabitants had to remain segregated from the rest of the local population for fear of spreading the plague in 1567.

It is a small community of approximately 200 people, where there is a definite 'village feel'. Everybody knows everybody – and their business!

There are no shops in Hepwood, only a local pub and a church. But there are many traditional events that take place during the year, such as garden fetes, vegetable shows and the annual Christmas fair in the Village Hall.

It is the home of local sculptor, Andrew Matthews, who has gained local fame for his wooden carvings. These can be seen dotted around the gardens of local homes.

Here are some of the technical terms that you would be expected to comment on in your response to an informative text such as this one.

- This piece of text is clearly factual, and its purpose is to give information about the village of Hepwood.
- The reader is presented with facts about Hepwood and its history and traditions.
- The language is simple so that it can be accessed by a wide audience – anyone who is interested in reading about the village.
- It is not trying to persuade people to visit; it simply tells them about the place. If it was trying to persuade the audience to visit, you would expect to see far more adjectives, describing the village's 'quaint feel' and 'pretty location'. The pub is merely referred to as that, not a '**quaint** English pub that serves **delicious** food'.
- The picture could be a persuasive feature, if the piece was to be persuasive, as it looks like an attractive village. However, here it merely adds further information in the form of a visual aid, so that the reader can see what the village looks like.

Persuasive Texts

Persuasive writing aims to persuade the reader to believe, think or do something.

As with all texts, a persuasive text might have a specific audience, and this is shown by the persuasive techniques used. For example, a text aimed at teenagers to persuade them to buy a certain phone or brand of trainers might use the kind of language that teenagers use.

Typical examples of writing to persuade (as the primary purpose) include:

- Holiday travel brochures.
- Charity leaflets, campaigns and web pages.
- Television, radio and web advertisements.
- Promotional materials for bands.
- Film, book and music promotional materials.
- Magazine articles.

Key Features of Writing to Persuade

Persuasive techniques include the use of **emotive adjectives**, e.g. 'cruel', 'beautiful', 'harsh' – descriptive words that have an impact on the reader and make them think or feel a certain response to the things being described.

Adverbs, such as 'cruelly', 'despicably' and 'carefully' are often used in persuasive writing. Adverbs describe actions in certain ways and reveal a lot about how things are done. They can affect the way in which the reader responds to the person doing the action. For example, in the sentence, 'The woman beat the child mercilessly', the adverb 'mercilessly' reveals that the woman was very cruel, and this makes the reader respond negatively towards her.

Adjectives and adverbs used in this way are examples of **emotive language** – words used to make the reader feel a certain way. Words such as 'cruel' and 'mercilessly' are also examples of the use of **negative diction**.

Negative diction (bad words) and **positive diction** (good words) are found in persuasive writing and are intended to make you feel a certain way. They indicate how the writer feels about the topic they are writing about. For example, if a writer described you as a 'charming, delightful and considerate individual' it would be safe to say that they liked you!

Bias and **opinion** are used a lot in persuasive writing to persuade, change or influence the reader's opinion. For example, if a writer says that something is 'horrible', they are making it clear that they do not like it. They are not being factual; they are simply offering their opinion in the hope that it might bias yours.

The **tone** of a text will reveal how the writer feels about the topic and the way that they want the reader to react to it. The tone of a persuasive text could be amusing/humorous, sarcastic, critical, factual, passionate, angry, serious, sad, etc.

Personal pronouns (e.g. 'I', 'you') are used a lot in persuasive texts to directly involve the reader and make them feel personally addressed. For example, if a writer states, 'How can we stand by and let this happen?', the collective 'we' is inviting the reader to get involved and do something about it. This is also a rhetorical question, which is a commonly used persuasive technique. It does not require an answer but it is used to get the reader to act or react.

Persuasive Texts

Exaggeration (or **hyperbole**) is used to give greater emphasis to something. Writers often use exaggeration, especially when the purpose of the writing is to persuade. Exaggeration includes the use of **superlatives**, for example, when the piece of writing states that something is 'the best', 'the greatest', 'the cleanest', 'the most effective', etc.

Exclamatory sentences usually end with an exclamation mark and are used to show shock, horror, disbelief, etc. They are often used in persuasive writing. For example, 'This is an outrage! It cannot be that expensive to bring up a child!'

Repetition is often used in persuasive writing to stress a word or a phrase to make it stick in the reader's mind. It might be a word or phrase that the writer wants the reader to notice and react towards. For example, 'Child poverty in this country is a disgrace; child poverty in this country is an embarrassment; child poverty in this country must be stopped now'. The **use of three** can be seen here, as well as repetition. Use of three is a technique used frequently by politicians and people delivering persuasive speeches.

Juxtaposition means placing things (words) side by side for comparison. For example, if a writer describes a dog that has been found abandoned by the roadside in sad terms, mentioning its thin state and its starved condition, but then describes it as being healthy and happy in the next paragraph, then juxtaposition has been used. By juxtaposing the sad and the happy sides of the story, the reader can see the difference clearly. This can be done just as effectively with images.

The above is not a complete list; many of the technical terms that are used in persuasive writing can be found in other sections of this guide. The ones listed here are some of the more commonly used techniques to persuade the reader.

Remember that topics in this revision guide are divided in a way that will help your revision, but they must be dealt with as a whole.

Preparation Task

You have already seen an example of writing to persuade on page 16. Have another look at it and see if you can spot some of these persuasive techniques in it.

Examples of Persuasive Texts

The following texts are examples of persuasive texts.

Which persuasive features can you find in them?

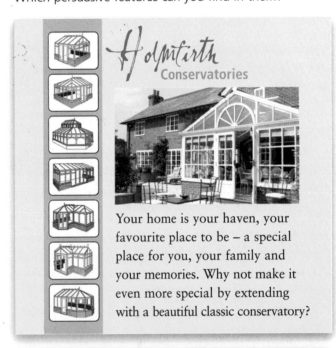

Your home is your haven, your favourite place to be – a special place for you, your family and your memories. Why not make it even more special by extending with a beautiful classic conservatory?

The great white shark is the most magnificent of creatures and it has been given some bad press in recent years. It is not the great killer of the deep that many would have us believe! In fact, researchers have proved that these superb creatures only ever attack humans when they mistake them for seals.

Helpful Hint

When you have read a text, think about your immediate reaction. How does it make you feel? If it makes you feel sad, outraged, delighted – or any strong emotion – you have probably just read a persuasive text.

Persuasive Texts – Presentational Devices

A persuasive text could be in the form of a letter, a book, a leaflet, an article in a newspaper or magazine, a web page, etc. This means that the **presentation** is very important.

The colours, font sizes and use of images can be very influential features of a persuasive text.

Newspapers, magazines, adverts and other texts use a variety of presentational devices, such as columns, colour and photos.

In questions about form and presentation, you need to consider three main points:
- The presentational devices that are used.
- The effect that they are intended to have on the reader.
- How successful you think the presentational devices are in affecting/influencing the reader.

You need to show the examiner that you understand *why* the presentational devices are effective. You need to show that you understand why various techniques have been used, for example, why a magazine article contains a certain photo, or why a report is laid out a certain way.

Presentational Devices

The following checklist gives you an idea of what to look out for when responding to persuasive and other non-fiction texts. It will also give you ideas of techniques that you could use when you are producing your own persuasive texts in the exam and when you are working on your controlled assessment tasks.

- **Images**, e.g. photographs, pictures, cartoons and diagrams. Analyse their position on the page and their appeal. What are they trying to achieve? What impact/effect are they trying to have on the reader? Look out for juxtaposition of images.
- **Illustrations**, e.g. graphs, maps and logos. Why have they been included? Are they persuasive or are they simply informative?
- **Image captions** – are they emotive, factual or humorous?
- **Colour** – look at the colours that are used. What feeling do the colours create? Has a particular colour been used deliberately because of its connotations (associations)? For example, red is associated with danger or death.
- **Headlines** – look for alliteration, wordplay, puns and humour.
- **Sub-headings** – are they really informative? Do they break up the text for the reader and give the piece some cohesion?
- **Font sizes** – large lettering, different fonts and different colours may be used. Which words or parts of the text do they emphasise?
- **Upper case letters** – capital letters are often used for key words to make them stand out.
- **Bold type, italics and underlining** – like upper case letters, they highlight certain words or topics.
- **Catchy titles/headings and slogans** – these are often used in adverts. What effect do they have?
- **Overall layout** – how is the piece presented? Why have magazine and newspaper articles been laid out in columns? Does the text have a border? Are parts of the text separated into boxes? What effect does this have?

Responding to Persuasive Texts

When responding to a persuasive text, the examiner wants to see that you can:

- Identify the purpose and audience.
- Identify the style techniques and presentational devices used to influence the reader.
- Compare the text with other texts.
- Discuss the effectiveness of the text.
- Identify bias (persuasion).

The PEE Technique

It can help you to organise your responses if you use **PEE**: Point, Evidence/Example, Explanation. (This technique is also known as PEC: Point, Evidence/Example, Comment, or as 123.)

P – Make a point

For example, '*The writer is trying to convince the reader that MP3 players pose a threat to young people's hearing.*'

E – Provide evidence/an example

For example, '*The cartoon image of the boy shows that he is in pain and the red haze at the top of his head suggests that the noise is painful.*'

E – Give an explanation

For example, '*The caption, 'How much fun is he having?' is used ironically. He does not look like he is having fun. The writer is trying to get the reader to see that the boy is in pain to make his point that MP3 players are bad for your hearing*'.

When responding to a text in the exam, you should:

- Read the text at least twice and highlight interesting language and presentational features.
- Jot down what you think the writer wanted to achieve by writing the piece.
- Consider what impact the writer wanted to have on the reader, and whether they achieve this.

Responding to Persuasive Texts

Persuasive texts aim to influence your opinion about something. Not all persuasive texts are obvious. They may use bias rather than out-and-out persuasion – there is a subtle difference. Bias can affect your thoughts and even make you want to change them, but it is about putting the writer's opinion across as much as it is about changing the reader's opinion. Purely persuasive texts just want to change your opinion.

Alongside is an example of how to respond to a persuasive text.

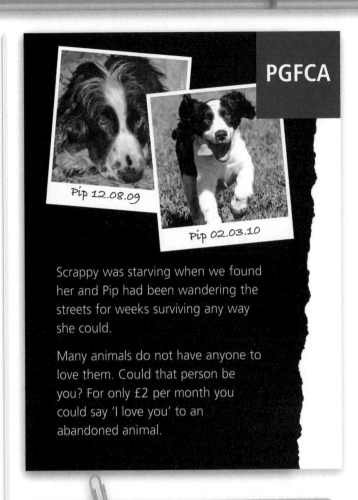

PGFCA

Pip 12.08.09

Pip 02.03.10

Scrappy was starving when we found her and Pip had been wandering the streets for weeks surviving any way she could.

Many animals do not have anyone to love them. Could that person be you? For only £2 per month you could say 'I love you' to an abandoned animal.

The verb 'starving' shows that the dog was close to starvation, not just hungry. This makes the reader feel sorry for the dog.

Simple, short sentences are used to get the points across in a straightforward manner – they are the facts. The facts are good at persuading us as they cannot be argued with and are upsetting.

The rhetorical question 'Could that person be you?' is effective as the writer directly addresses the reader and involves them in the story.

Alliteration is used, 'abandoned animal' - it stresses the words that the writer wants the reader to respond to.

The juxtaposition of the photos gains the readers' attention and sympathy for the poor animal, whilst showing Pip looking healthy as a result of the intervention of the charity. So juxtaposition is used effectively to show the impact that giving money to the charity could have.

Analysing Persuasive Features

In the exam you will be expected to recognise that the primary purpose of a text might be to persuade. But you must remember that it will not only be persuasive pieces that use persuasive devices. For example, newspaper articles are factual pieces but they contain persuasive features.

It is important to remember that a piece of writing will not just have one type of writing within it, but many. Non-fiction texts can come in many forms and have elements of the different types of writing within them. You must be able to recognise the various techniques and their effects.

Fact and Opinion

Facts are statements that we can prove; **opinions** are personal views. Opinions can be persuasive. Look out for opinions given in texts and make sure you can distinguish when the writer is giving their opinion in order to persuade the reader, and when the writer is simply giving their opinion.

How to Spot Opinion

Certain words signal opinion. For example, the use of **adjectives** often signifies opinion rather than fact. Words such as 'seem', 'appear', 'suggest', 'might', 'may', 'should', 'could', 'would', 'supposedly', 'possibly', 'believe', 'apparently' and 'allegedly', also imply opinion not fact.

Remember that writers often use **exaggeration** in order to persuade or to create a reaction in the reader. This often includes the use of **superlatives** (words such as 'best', 'greatest', 'nicest', and the use of 'most …' as in 'most fantastic'). Superlatives often suggest someone's opinion.

Look at example 1 opposite. Because a number has been used, you may think it is fact. Yet how do we know that the offers are 'fantastic'? This is just someone's opinion; other people might think they are far from 'fantastic'.

Look at example 2. This is fact because the statement can be checked and proved. It is not just someone's opinion.

Look at example 3, a shop sale sign. Not everyone will agree that the sale is the 'best ever' and no one will ever be able to prove this extravagant claim, which makes this text opinion, not fact.

Read example 4. The first two sentences are facts, as they can be checked and proven to be true. However, the final sentence is opinion. The adjectives 'worrying' and 'disgraceful' convey the writer's views rather than actual fact.

These are good examples of texts having a variety of language features and more than one purpose.

① 5 FANTASTIC OFFERS!

② UP TO £500 OFF SELECTED MODELS

③ BEST EVER SALE!

④ *Safety Assured*

'When we test cars we always check the security of doors. In this report we reveal our findings. It adds up to a worrying picture for car owners and a disgraceful one for car manufacturers'.

Analysing Persuasive Features – Example

The following text is the type of text that you could get in the exam. It is a **biography**. It is not a persuasive text, but many persuasive features can be found in it. For example, opinion, adjectives, and use of three.

Study this extract taken from William M. Thayer's biography *Abraham Lincoln*. Abraham Lincoln was President of the USA from 1861 to 1865.
Here is an example of the sort of question you could be asked on a non-fiction text like this one.

The miserable log cabin in which Abraham Lincoln was born was a floorless, doorless, windowless shanty, situated in one of the most barren and desolate spots of Hardin County, Kentucky. His father made it his home simply because he was too poor to own a better one. Nor was his an exceptional case of penury and want. For the people of that section were generally poor and unlettered, barely able to scrape enough together to keep the wolf of hunger from their abodes.

Here Abraham Lincoln was born February 12th, 1809. His father's name was Thomas Lincoln; his mother's maiden name was Nancy Hanks… They had been married three years when Abraham was born. Their cabin was in that part of Hardin County which is now embraced in La Rue County, a few miles from Hodgensville – on the south fork of Nolin Creek. A perennial spring of water, gushing in silvery brightness from beneath a rock near by, relieved the barrenness of the location, and won for it the somewhat ambitious name – "Rock Spring Farm."

Q How does Thayer use language to convey the place where Abraham Lincoln was born?

The following are some points you might decide to write about in your answer to the question above.

- Negative phrases in the first paragraph suggest a difficult life in poor conditions, e.g. 'miserable log cabin', 'floorless…shanty'. These negative phrases emphasise Lincoln's humble start in life compared to him becoming President later in life and therefore having everything.
- Adjectives in the first paragraph help to create an image in the reader's mind of the poor living conditions Lincoln was born into, e.g. 'miserable', 'barren', 'desolate'.
- Use of three in 'floorless, doorless, windowless shanty' highlights the bad points of Lincoln's childhood home.
- Rhyme of 'floorless, doorless' makes these negative adjectives stand out.
- Metaphors, e.g. 'wolf of hunger'. This provides a vivid image of the fear of starvation.
- The second paragraph becomes more informative giving clear facts about Lincoln's parents.
- Phrases in the second paragraph are more positive than in the first, e.g. 'which is now embraced in…'. These positive words and phrases imply a happy life, despite the problems of where the family lived.
- Onomatopoeia is used, e.g. 'gushing', to highlight the fact that the water is the best thing about the location.
- The metaphor in the third paragraph is also more positive, e.g. 'gushing in silvery brightness'. This also suggests some beauty in the 'barrenness of the location'.

Helpful Hint

Note how many of the language terms that you have come across so far in the book can be applied here. It is important that you use the terms appropriately.

 # THE WEEKLY NEWS

Flash Floods Devastate Local Villages

Homes, businesses and lives ruined as flood water rises

Flash floods devastated villages in Derbyshire overnight on Friday. The full extent of the destruction is not yet known, but one thing is for certain: repairing the damaged property and getting people's lives back to normal could take months, if not years.

Destruction

One victim of the floods was Charlie Turner, 54, from Leafdale. He awoke on Saturday morning to find his home swamped under a metre of water. But there was more terrible news waiting for him in nearby Greenham when he went to open up the family business, Charlie's Chippie. He found flood water halfway up the walls and his deep-fat fryers completely submerged. Says Charlie, 'My grandfather Charlie opened this chippie in 1960 and we've been open 6 days a week ever since. I feel like

I'm letting down the family name by having to close up'. Charlie's life has been devastated by the flood and it will take him many months to repair the damage.

Widespread damage

Every villager in Leafdale has a similar story to tell, and although the weather is due to ease this week, this is no consolation to the many whose homes and businesses have already been ruined. Single mum-of-two Anna Grayson said, 'I just don't know where to start. We're going to have to stay at my mum's until the repair work can be done on the house. It's just a dreadful situation'.

Study the newspaper article above. Despite being primarily an informative text, it uses many persuasive devices.

Here is an example of the sort of question you could be asked on a non-fiction text like this one.

Q **Write about the features of the newspaper article that make the reader feel sympathetic.**

The following are some points you might decide to write about in your answer to the question above.

- The headline uses alliteration in 'flash floods' to highlight the main point of the article. The use of the word 'flash' also implies that it happened so quickly the villagers weren't prepared for it.
- Use of three in the strapline ('Homes, businesses and lives') emphasises the damage caused by the flood.
- Sensational words are used throughout the article for effect, e.g. 'destruction', 'terrible', 'devastated'.
- Emotive words are used in the article, for example, 'victim'.
- Use of 'single mum-of-two' lets readers identify and sympathise with the woman's situation.

- The fact that the article uses quotes from people who have been affected by the flood makes it seem more real, and allows the reader to identify with the situation the people face.
- The article focuses in particular on one 'victim of the floods' whose home and business have been damaged. This highlights the extent of the flood damage. A quote from this man is used, which talks about how long his business has been going and how it was founded by his grandfather. This gains sympathy by stressing the family connection.
- Opinion is used by the writer to sound like fact, e.g. 'repairing the damaged property... could take months'. This again highlights the extent of the damage and suggests that the people will suffer for a long time.

Helpful Hint

In the examination you may use the PEE technique in more detail than is done here to show that you can write about the effect of language on the reader.

Producing Non-fiction Texts

Unit 1: Understanding and Producing Non-fiction Texts

Section B – Writing

At both Foundation Tier and Higher Tier, you must do two compulsory writing tasks:

- One short task worth 16 marks.
- One longer task worth 24 marks.

The writing tasks will be based on a range of non-fiction genres. All tasks will ask candidates to write for specific audiences and purposes, adapting their style so that it is fit for purpose.

What is the Examiner Looking For?

The examiner wants to know that you can write accurately and appropriately in English. Regardless of which question you choose to answer the examiner will always be looking for the same things. You need to make sure that you can do the following:

- Communicate and express your ideas clearly in writing.
- Organise ideas into sentences, paragraphs and whole texts, and try to use a variety of sentence structures.
- Punctuate accurately with commas, full stops, apostrophes, etc., and spell words correctly.

- Use vocabulary 'for effect'; do not always choose the most simple and obvious words, but think carefully about the meaning you want to put across.
- Write effectively in different forms (e.g. letters, leaflets).
- Write for a particular purpose and audience.
- Make the purpose of your writing clear.
- Keep the reader interested in what you say and how you say it by communicating effectively and using a variety of appropriate language techniques.

When you are writing non-fiction texts, you need to remember all the techniques that you have revised. For example, when writing persuasively, you need to remember to use the techniques you noticed when responding to persuasive texts.

Helpful Hint

The key things to remember when producing non-fiction texts can be remembered by using the the mnemonic FLAP:

- form (genre) and presentational devices
- language/style
- audience
- purpose

Form and Presentation

Every piece of writing has a particular **form** or **genre**. The form is how the writing is presented.

In this section of the exam, you are often asked to write in a particular form or genre. Here are some examples of genres that you could be asked to write:

- Holiday brochure extracts.
- Newspaper reports.
- Magazine articles.
- Informal or formal letters.
- Leaflets.
- Advice sheets.
- News sheets.
- Memos.
- On-line pages/emails.

Form and Genre

Make sure that you use the right form and that you apply the correct conventions for that form. For example, if you were asked to write a newspaper article, you would need to include a headline and a strapline. If you are asked to design a persuasive web page for a charity, think about the way that this would be set out on the page.

You cannot create a real web page in the exam, but you can include notes at the side of your text to show where you would include a picture or change the colour, and explain briefly why you would do this and the effect that it would have on the reader.

Presentational Devices

In the exam you might decide that the text you are creating would include a picture. You do not have to spend valuable writing time drawing a picture – a small explanation describing what you would have in the picture and why is fine. The same techniques can be used for diagrams or graphs.

You could do the same to indicate font sizes and colours: draw an arrow pointing to words that you would change into a different font and different colours.

Helpful Hint

Note that in the controlled assessments, you may want to actually produce the text that you are creating as you want it to look. Unlike in the exam, you will have time to use real pictures and different font sizes and colours when doing your controlled assignment.

Audience and Purpose

Before you start to write, you need to consider:

- **The audience**
  Who are you writing for? Do you know the person? How old is he/she?
- **The purpose of the writing**
  What are you trying to achieve through the writing?

Audience

There are many different audiences for whom you may be asked to write. Here are some examples:

- Teenagers.
- Adults.
- Children.
- Football fans.
- The local council.
- Pupils at your school.
- Teachers.

Make sure that you use the appropriate language, style, presentational devices and layout for your audience. If your text is a formal text, like a letter, use formal, Standard English. If your text is aimed at teenagers you could use teenage language if that is appropriate to the type of writing that you are doing.

Some texts are formal and some can be written informally. It depends on your audience and where the text would be read. A teenagers' magazine might use informal language, but an adults' Sunday supplement from a newspaper might require formal language.

Purpose

In this section of the exam, you may be asked to:

- **Argue** for or against something.
- **Persuade** someone to do or not to do something.
- **Advise** someone on the best, easiest, quickest or most effective way to do something.
- **Inform** someone about something.

You may be asked to write a text that combines two or more of these purposes.

Make sure you understand the purpose of what you are being asked to write. Read the task that you are set very carefully.

Choose to write a text that you feel comfortable with and know how to do.

Helpful Hint

Make sure you consider the purpose of your text and the audience when you are writing your own texts in the exam (or in the controlled assessment). The purpose may be to persuade or inform. The audience may be quite general, e.g. teenagers, or quite specific, e.g. dog owners. Keep both the purpose and audience in your mind as you write to ensure that you use the appropriate language and style.

If the question you choose to answer does not state a specific audience, write as you would when you write an essay; keep your language quite formal and avoid using the personal pronoun 'you' too much, as you cannot address your audience directly when you do not know who they are.

Language and Style

You need to use appropriate language for the text that you are writing. The words and techniques that you use show the examiner that you understand that particular type of writing and can use the techniques that are expected of this genre.

The language you use in your writing should be appropriate for the audience you are aiming at, so you need to make sure you adopt the right **register** (tone).

Register is the tone of voice and the level of formality you use when speaking and writing. You wouldn't speak to your teachers in the same way you speak to your brothers and sisters, so the register needs to be chosen carefully. The audience is the main thing that influences your choice of register, however, the purpose and form will also affect the type of language you use.

For example, imagine there is a huge party on Friday night. But there is one big problem – it is during your exams and your teacher is sending letters home telling everyone they must stay in and revise.

> **Q** **Write a letter to your teacher persuading her to let you go to the party.**

What form, language, audience and purpose are needed for this piece of writing? Start by underlining the clues that are in the question. Your question would then look something like this:

> **Q** **Write a <u>letter</u> to your <u>teacher</u> <u>persuading</u> her to let you go to the party.**

So now you have the form, audience and purpose. The form, audience and purpose tell you which type of language to use so if you are using the FLAP mnemonic to help you, fill in the language section last.

Form (Genre) – letter
Language – formal (it's to your teacher, not your friend!)
Audience – your teacher
Purpose – persuade

Preparation Task

Underline the key words in the following question and then use the FLAP technique to identify the form, language, audience and purpose.

> **Q** **Write a speech to be made at a governors' meeting where you, as a student, try to persuade the governors to abolish school uniform.**

30

Writing for a Particular Audience

Whatever you are writing, it is essential that you think about the audience for whom you are writing the text. You must ask yourself, 'who is going to read this?'. This will help you to use the right language.

An audience could be:

- Adults.
- Children.
- Teenagers.
- Older retired people.
- Boys.
- Girls.
- Men.
- Women.
- People with a specific interest, e.g. bird watchers, athletes.

However, some audiences are very varied so some texts need to appeal to a **general audience**. For example, think about all the different people who will read a newspaper in a day. The differences between them will be massive: they will have different jobs, different interests and will lead very different lives. Writers need to take this into account when writing their pieces.

On the other hand, some newspapers target certain readers. For example, it is supposed that higher earning, educated people read broadsheet newspapers like *The Times* and *The Independent*. The tabloids are traditionally read more by working-class, less well-educated readers. Newspapers such as *The Sun*, *Daily Mirror* and *Daily Star* have a lower required reading age than the broadsheets (i.e. the language and sentence structure is simple, so younger people are able to read and understand them). The language used in broadsheets is more complex, as are the sentence structures and length of the articles.

Writing for Different Audiences

Here are some general rules to bear in mind when writing for different audiences. But remember that the purpose and form will also affect the language you use.

Audience	Use:
Adults	More complex vocabulary, longer sentences, more difficult subject matter, smaller font size, longer articles, formal tone, Standard English.
Children	Simple vocabulary, shorter sentences, larger font size, shorter articles, pictures to keep them interested.
Teenagers	'Trendy' language, colloquial and slang vocabulary, informal register and tone, humour.
Men	Traditionally/stereotypically 'masculine' words and topics.
Women	Traditionally/stereotypically 'feminine' words and topics.

Preparation Task

Find two articles about the same topic – one from a broadsheet newspaper and one from a tabloid newspaper – and carry out your own language study. In what ways do the newspapers write the stories differently?

Consider:

- The length of the articles, and number of paragraphs.
- Headlines.
- Sentence length and complexity.
- Register and tone, and vocabulary used.
- Use of quotes and pictures.

Helpful Hints

Researching and studying articles from different types of newspapers will be useful for writing your own newspaper articles in the exam or as a controlled assessment task.

Beware of stereotyping people/audiences. We can only ever make generalisations about people – stereotypes are not necessarily true.

Writing Persuasive Texts

When you are writing persuasively, you need to remember all the techniques that you have revised about responding to persuasive texts. You must try to use the same techniques in your own writing.

Persuading involves getting your readers to agree with a point of view, or making them feel a certain way. This might involve argument, but it will usually also involve other methods of trying to influence people's feelings. You must:

- Try to make someone do something they might not want to do.
- Understand why they might not want to do this.
- Use different techniques to try to persuade them.

Techniques for Writing to Persuade

The following are some of the techniques that are effective in persuasive writing. You should use some of these when writing a persuasive piece.

- **Positive or negative vocabulary** to influence your reader's opinion.
- **Repetition** or **use of three** to emphasise your main points.
- **Direct personal address** to the reader to make them feel more involved, e.g. the use of the personal pronoun 'you'.

- **Rhetorical questions** to force the reader to question the issue.
- **Evidence and justification** (e.g. this happened because…') give structure and reasoning to your opinion (use the **PEE technique**).
- **Comparative devices** like **similes** and **metaphors** emphasise your main points.
- A **conclusion** that links to the introduction and summarises the main points in your piece of writing.

These kinds of techniques are frequently used in persuasive writing such as letters, adverts and speeches.

The letter below is an example of persuasive writing.

Practice Question

Q **Write a leaflet to persuade pupils at your school to take part in a 5km fun run for charity. You could talk about:**
- **Why pupils should take part.**
- **The charity involved and the benefits to the charity.**

Opening statement grabs audience's attention	19 Clark Close Oaklee
Suitable connective links the sentences	Weekly News 15 High Street Oaklee Dear Editor,
Acknowledging a different view	I am writing to you to voice my opposition to the building of a supermarket on the village recreation ground. Although I am strongly against this proposal I do recognise that there are some equally important issues about the lack of a supermarket in the village that need addressing.
Suitable connectives open the paragraphs	Firstly, if a supermarket was built it would completely destroy the recreation ground. Where would we hold our annual show? Where would the cricket team play? Where would the children play? In times of rising obesity levels, I think we need more space for our children to play, not another retail outlet selling junk food.
Rhetorical questions and use of three	
Evidence and justification of writer's opinion	Secondly, our village has a very busy market and village shopping centre. If a supermarket was built, no one would shop here anymore and people would lose jobs. I appreciate that a supermarket would create some jobs but not as many as those lost.
Present tense makes the issue seem more immediate	I agree that parking is a problem in the village and that the small village shops are expensive compared to out-of-town supermarkets. Perhaps the council could put on a free bus once a week to the large supermarket.
Clear concluding paragraph which links to the introduction and summarises the main points	In conclusion, I feel that the recreation ground is vital to village life in many ways and whilst the problem of access to supermarkets does need addressing, this cannot be at the expense of village life. Yours faithfully *E Burton* Mrs Eileen Burton

Writing Informative Texts

Writing to inform (i.e. give information) is when you create a text that teaches, tells or informs the reader about a topic.

You are not trying to persuade them to do something; you are simply teaching, or telling, them about something.

When writing to inform, you must:
- Present the readers with a clear set of facts.
- Communicate the facts in a way that is easy for the readers to understand.
- Write from an unbiased point of view.

The letter below, from a headteacher to parents, is an example of writing to inform. It informs the reader what will happen; the writer does not have to argue a case or persuade the reader, but may go on to explain certain things in more detail.

Wadefield High School

Dear Parent / Guardian,

I am writing to inform you about some important events in the coming term. Year 11 pupils will commence study leave on 20 May. Half term will be from Monday 29 May until Friday 2 June. Monday 5 June will be an INSET day for the staff.

Wadefield High School, 115 Broad Street, Upperthong, Wadefield WD1 1TT
t: 01924 683377 **f:** 01924 683378 **e:** wadefieldhighschool@co.uk

Helpful Hint

If the purpose of the writing is to inform, focus on who, what, where and when.

Writing to Inform

Informative texts can take many forms, for example, letters, articles and leaflets. However, don't assume that all letters, articles and leaflets are informative – remember they may be persuasive or they may advise the reader, or they may have more than one purpose. For example, a leaflet aimed at teenagers encouraging them not to take drugs would be persuasive, but it would also include facts about drugs.

Here are some examples of the type of questions you could get in this section of the exam:

Q **Write a letter to your MP informing him / her about what it is like to be a young person living in your area.**
Remember to:
- **Write in the form of a letter.**
- **Use language suitable for an MP.**
- **Inform the MP.**

Q **People often find it difficult to understand why others spend their leisure time in the way they do. Write informatively about your favourite leisure pursuit.**

In these two questions you are asked to write about experiences. To write in an interesting way about these experiences you might need to explain why or how things happen, and give your own feelings and opinions, but the emphasis is on informing. You could even be asked to inform people about something personal, such as a forthcoming wedding, but you still need to focus on informing.

Creating Leaflets

You may be asked to write the text for a leaflet or information sheet. This is usually to inform or persuade. You will need to use all the devices covered in this chapter. You may get a question such as this:

Q Write the text for a leaflet written by an environmental group who focus on the need to recycle. Try to persuade teenagers to join this environmental group.

Leaflets usually contain a mixture of facts and opinions. A fact is something that can be proven to be true. An opinion is someone's viewpoint. (See page 24.)

Techniques for Writing Leaflets

- Plan your leaflet with your audience in mind.
- Create an effective headline.
- Your first paragraph should catch the reader's attention.
- Sub-headings can guide the reader through the text and lead them to important points.
- Bullet points and text boxes are often used in leaflets, but remember this is an English writing exam – you will not get full marks if you only use bullet points.
- Use a mixture of fact and opinion.

Presentational Devices

Leaflets often have:
- Covers and titles.
- Introductory paragraphs.
- Concluding paragraphs.
- Different font sizes and colours.
- Headings and sub-headings to break up information for the reader.
- Images and pictures.
- Clear paragraphs.

You will not be expected in the exam to spend time on presentational devices, other than simple headings and sub-headings (and perhaps bullet points or a numbered list). Do not waste time on drawings.

A leaflet is often a sheet of A4 paper that has been folded to make it more noticeable/interesting. In the exam you are not expected to fold your leaflet. Folding your answer paper may confuse the examiner and could make your writing more difficult to follow.

The text on leaflets is often written in columns. Some students confuse columns with paragraphs. Remember that a column is a vertical presentational device whereas a paragraph is a horizontal organisational device.

Writing Texts to Advise

Writing to advise means you taking on the role of the expert, as you will be telling someone else the best, easiest or quickest way to do something.

The following points show the main things to remember when you are writing to advise:

A – Advice must be clear.
D – Do keep in role.
V – Vocabulary should include modal verbs (e.g. 'can', 'would').
I – Informal but polite.
C – Choices must be given.
E – Encourage and motivate.

Techniques in Writing to Advise

The suggestions below are words and phrases you may find effective to use when you are writing to advise. A selection of useful phrases is given here for each of the points shown above:

- **Advice must be clear**
    - You need to follow these three steps…
    - The first thing to do is…
    - The next step…
    - Finally…

- **Do keep in role**
    - It is my professional opinion that…
    - Many people come to me for advice…

- **Vocabulary should include modal verbs**
    - 'can', 'will', 'shall', 'may', 'could', 'would', 'should', 'might', 'must', 'ought'.

- **Informal but polite**
    - Get your friends to help you…
    - Good luck…
    - Don't panic…

- **Choices must be given**
    - You should talk to your parents or another adult…
    - Alternatively…
    - If this doesn't work then…

- **Encourage and motivate**
    - Things may seem bad but don't worry…
    - You can do this…
    - You can be successful if you…
    - I believe we can achieve anything…

The response to the letter alongside is an example of writing to advise.

asksam

I am a 15 year old girl studying for my GCSEs. These exams are very important to me as I want to go to university and train to be a solicitor so I'm working really hard for them.

My friends make fun of me. They say I work all the time and call me a swot and a geek. I don't want to lose my friends but I need to do well in my exams.

What should I do?

Claire, London.

Advice:

I really sympathise with you Claire: things may seem bad, but don't worry. Clearly your friends are not as sensible as you and are not taking their exams as seriously as they ought to be. Have you talked to them about how important these exams are? Many people believe that GCSE grades will determine what you do for the rest of your life. You could try explaining to your friends how important it is for you to do well. Tell them your ambitions for the future and that you'd like them to support you. Alternatively, try getting them to help you – you could set up a revision club. If these ideas don't work then it might be that the people you call your friends are not really true friends. I think you should concentrate on your own future – you might not even know your friends in two years' time. You can be successful and get into your dream job if you work hard enough for your exams.

Good luck!

Encouraging phrases which offer sympathy	Informal and friendly tone
Suitable connectives	Giving choices
Modal verbs	Keeping role as an expert
Introducing evidence	Phrase to encourage and motivate

Planning Your Writing

In your exam you should spend about five minutes planning your answer. You will not get any extra marks for planning but it will help you to write organised and well-structured pieces which will, in turn, help you to get a higher grade. A plan will ensure that you discuss every subject you want to cover in a logical, sensible order; this will make your piece of writing better.

There are a number of ways to plan your answer; the most common techniques are shown here as responses to the following question:

Q **Write a letter to the school governors to try to persuade them to abolish school uniform.**

Brainstorm

Brainstorming your ideas or using a 'mind map' is an easy but effective way to plan.

Paragraph 1
Why uniform is bad
- Everyone looks the same
- Ties are dangerous
- Uncomfortable

Paragraph 2
Why uniform is good
- Looks tidy
- Poorer pupils can afford it
- Makes you feel part of school

LETTER TO GOVERNORS

Paragraph 3
Why the above is wrong
- Everyone tries to make it look different
- Everyone still knows who the poor kids are
- Shouldn't need uniform to make you feel like you belong

Conclusion
- Europe does not have uniform
- This is the 21st century – people can be more individual

A List

A list is a simple and clear way to plan what you are going to say.

LETTER TO GOVERNORS

Paragraph 1: Uniform is bad

- Everyone looks the same
- Ties are dangerous
- Uncomfortable

Paragraph 2: Uniform is good

- Looks tidy
- Poorer pupils can afford it
- Makes you feel part of school

Paragraph 3: Why the above is wrong

- Everyone tries to make it look different
- Still know who the poor kids are
- Shouldn't need uniform to make you feel like you belong

Conclusion

- Europe does not have uniform
- This is the 21st century – people can be more individual

Planning Your Writing

A Writing Frame

Many students find writing frames helpful. They are just another way of organising your thoughts using key phrases in each section. So, for your introduction in a letter you may write something like 'I am writing to you today…'.

Date

Address

Dear

On behalf of the school council, I am writing…

We feel very strongly about this issue.

Although I recognise that there are some arguments against my proposals…

However I feel that…

I hope, therefore, that you can offer your support…

Yours…

Preparation Task

Read the following question and make a plan in one of the three ways shown here. You could try making a plan in each of the three ways shown to decide which technique works best for you.

Q **Write a letter to a local newspaper in which you persuade the council to provide more recycling facilities in the local area.**

Helpful Hint

Give yourself about five minutes in the exam to plan your answer, but do not take much longer than this; the plan will not count towards your mark so make sure you spend enough time actually writing your answer.

You do not have to stick rigidly to your plan. If you find whilst you are writing your answer that you want to add something, leave something out, or swap the order around, straying from the plan will not affect your mark.

It does not matter which technique you use to plan your answer, as long as you plan.

Practice Questions

Complete the two tasks on this spread. Give yourself 1 hour in which to answer both of them.

Writing Tips

Useful Words and Phrases for Your Own Writing

There are certain words and phrases that can be very useful in writing to argue, persuade or advise. Some of these words and phrases are given here with descriptions of how and when you should use them.

- **To state your opinions:** these phrases indicate that what follows is your personal opinion. They are polite and quite formal, and are, therefore, useful in letters and speeches.
  - I feel / think / consider…
  - In my opinion…
  - I am convinced that…

- **To link your ideas / opinions:** these connectives (see page 80) make your writing flow well.
  - Firstly…
  - Secondly…
  - In addition…
  - A further consideration must be…
  - Similarly…

- **To introduce evidence:** these phrases can be useful in backing up your idea or opinion.
  - It has come to my attention that…
  - A recent survey in the school newspaper found that…

- **To give the alternative view:** these phrases help to justify your opinion, by implying that other people have the same opinion as you.
  - Some people have said that…
  - Some people believe that…
  - Many people think…

- **To present a balanced view:** these connectives suggest that a new idea / opinion will follow. They are used when one idea / opinion has been discussed, and a new one is being introduced.
  - However…
  - On the other hand…
  - Nevertheless…

- **To be convincing (but polite):** these phrases show that you accept that other opinions can be valid.
  - Clearly some people will have opposing views, but I believe…
  - I understand your objections…
  - I am sure you will agree that…

- **To discredit the other opinion:** these phrases suggest that there is evidence to prove that the other opinion / idea is wrong and that an explanation will follow to say why it is wrong.
  - Clearly, this is not true…
  - However, this is not the case…
  - This is misleading…

Checking your Work

You should spend five minutes of your time in the exam checking your answer. It is easy to make mistakes with spelling, punctuation and grammar when you are under pressure so it is important to read through your answer carefully when you have finished it.

Make sure you have:
- Used paragraphs and linked them with suitable connectives (see page 80).
- Used a variety of punctuation correctly.
- Spelt words correctly.
- Crossed out any mistakes neatly and written your corrections so that the examiner can clearly understand your intentions.

Speaking and Listening

Unit 2: Speaking and Listening

Controlled Assessment

Unit 2 of the exam is worth 20% of your overall marks. For Unit 2 you will be assessed on three activities. These activities will test your skills in:

- **Presenting.**
- **Discussing and listening.**
- **Role playing.**

Presenting

For the presenting part of the Unit 2 controlled assessment, you need to show that you can:

- Speak clearly.
- Structure a talk and keep it going.
- Use Standard English (see page 40).
- Address the audience appropriately (using the right language for the audience that you are addressing).

To get a C grade or above you need to show the assessor (your teacher) that you can:

- Convey information, ideas and feelings clearly and confidently.
- Emphasise significant points that you are trying to make.
- Use appropriate language to the audience and do this for a range of talks and situations.
- Use Standard English vocabulary and grammar (not slang or colloquial language).

Discussing and Listening

For the discussing and listening part of the Unit 2 controlled assessment, you need to show that you can:

- Listen to others and respond appropriately to their ideas.
- See other people's points of view and respond to them.
- Express your opinions clearly, and with structure (rather than just shouting, 'I don't agree!').

To get a C grade or above you need to show the assessor (your teacher) that you can:

- Challenge, develop and respond to what you hear in a fluent way, asking appropriate questions to seek the answers that you need.
- Analyse and reflect (think about) other people's ideas and opinions and keep the discussion going.
- Make good contributions to discussions that keep the discussion going in a positive way.

Role Playing

For the role play part of the Unit 2 controlled assessment, you need to show that you can:

- Act and respond like a given character.
- Take on the role that you have been given.
- Create a role appropriate to the task.

You might be asked to take on the role of a character in one of the texts that you have read, and you must act and respond as they would in order to show that you understand the character and what motivates them to act the way they do.

To get a C grade or above you need to show the assessor (your teacher) that you can:

- Create convincing characters using verbal and non-verbal techniques that you have chosen to use for a reason.
- Respond skilfully and sensitively in different situations.
- Explore issues, relationships and ideas whilst you are in role.

If you are following the English Language course, the skills that you acquire in preparing for these speaking and listening tasks will come in useful for your Spoken Language Study in Unit 3 of the exam (see pages 82–95.)

Helpful Hint

Each of the three activities is worth the same amount of marks so you need to work just as hard on all three. If you know that you are weaker in one of the areas, make sure that you gain as many marks as you can in the other tasks.

Standard English

What is Standard English?

Standard English is the variety of the English language that is classed by many as the 'correct' form of English. It is considered to be the right way to use English.

Standard English is a dialect. It does not have any regional variations, which are considered by some to be ungrammatical or non-standard English.

Standard English is used in formal situations. It is used in the media and by public figures, such as politicians, so it has prestige (i.e. respect and admiration) and is regarded by many as the most desirable form of English.

Standard English is what you are taught to use at school in your written work. Your teacher may have corrected you for using slang instead of Standard English in your work. For example, you may have written:
- 'Me and my mates went to town', **or**
- 'Where's (where is) the shops?'

If you used Standard English, you would write:
- 'My friends and I went to town', **and**
- 'Where are the shops?'

People often think that Standard English is 'posh English' and that only 'posh people' use it. This idea is wrong. This entire revision guide is written in Standard English and so are many of the texts in it.

In both the written and spoken elements of your course, you must show that you can use Standard English.

Speech and Writing

Writing is the form that most commonly uses Standard English. When you are writing in an exam or writing a letter or job application, for example, you must be able to use Standard English. However, when you are talking to your family and friends, you will probably use slang and colloquial English – informal language is used.

Spontaneous speech (when you speak without thinking about it or planning it) tends to use less standard forms. But some speech uses Standard English. For example, **planned speech** (when you write down what you want to say beforehand, e.g. for an assembly or presentation) often uses Standard English because it is delivered in a formal situation for an audience that you might not know.

However, if your audience was teenagers and you wanted to engage them (get them to listen), you might write the speech first, but still use some informal language and colloquial terms. This would engage your audience and get them to relate to you. In a job interview (i.e. a formal situation) you would use Standard English to show that you can communicate with a wide range of people.

Received Pronunciation

Received Pronunciation (RP) is often the way in which Standard English is spoken. Received Pronunciation is an **accent**. It does not have any regional variations. It is the way that people speak when they do not have a regional accent. You cannot tell which part of the country they come from.

Does your mum or dad have a 'telephone voice' or a 'posher' way of speaking with strangers? If so, they are probably trying to speak using Received Pronunciation.

Many of the newsreaders who read the national news on television use Received Pronunciation.

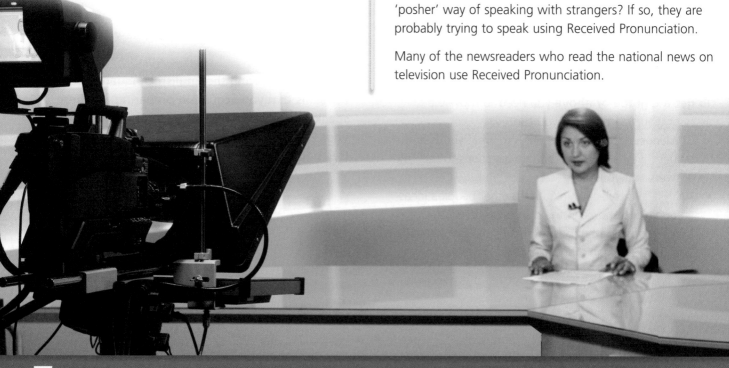

Non-standard Variations of English

Non-standard Variations of English

Non-standard variations of English are forms of English that do not follow the standard pattern. They are regional dialects and accents, i.e. ways of using English that have formed in different areas of the country.

Non-standard Dialects

Dialect refers to the words that are used and the grammatical way in which sentences are put together. Different dialectal words and sentence constructions are used in different regions of the country. For example:

– *'I ain't never done nothin' like that.'*
 (Non-Standard English)
– *'I have never done anything like that'.*
 (Standard English)

Note that:
- The words used are different.
- The order of the words (**syntax**) is different.

In the past, Standard English dialect and Received Pronunciation accent were considered 'better' English than non-standard forms and dialectal versions of English. Now, non-standard forms are referred to as **variations**, and are not regarded as inferior.

Non-standard Accents

There are many different accents used across the country. If you live in Liverpool, you probably sound different to people who live in Bristol or Edinburgh. This is because you have a different **accent**.

If you live in the south of England, you might pronounce words like 'bath', 'dance' and 'castle' with the long vowel in the word 'calm'. However, if you live in the midlands or the north, you might pronounce these words with the short vowel used in the word 'cat'.

Think about the continuous dramas/ soaps: *Coronation Street*, *EastEnders*, *Hollyoaks* and *Emmerdale*. The characters in these programmes sound different because the programmes are set in different parts of the country.

Other Factors Affecting Language

Where people live/come from is perhaps the main factor that affects the language they use, but other factors also influence language. For example:
- Social group.
- Age.
- Education and occupation.
- Gender.
- Culture.

Helpful Hint

In texts written in the past, the language the characters use can tell you a lot about them. Authors used to use dialectal variations and accents to show that characters were less educated or from a lower social group. Look out for examples of this in texts that you are studying.

Adapting Language

Effective Communication

It is important to be able to adapt language to make it appropriate for the context. You must consider:

- **Form / genre** – is it spoken or written, letter or newspaper article?
- **Language** – the style used.
- **Audience** – who is it aimed at?
- **Purpose** – what are you trying to do? Advise, persuade, instruct, inform?

Other factors also affect the language that we use, such as social group, age, education, occupation, gender, background and culture.

You can only use language and communicate effectively in both your speech and writing if you are aware of these features. For example, you would not use rap music language to talk to your grandmother, would you? If you did, she would not know what you were talking about! You need to adapt your language for a different audience, form or purpose.

Language Change

Language changes over time, and attitudes to the way that we use language changes over time. Some words have changed in meaning over time, whilst some words that we use today were not around many years ago – usually because the things they refer to were not invented then. For example:

- 'Internet' – a new invention, so a new word.
- 'Sad' – used to just mean 'upset'; now also means 'uncool'.
- 'Sick' – used to just mean 'ill', but now also means 'brilliant'.

The list is endless – it is a wonder that different generations of society can communicate at all!

Examples of Adapting Language

Example 1

If you were adapting a poem to a playscript, you would have to change:

- **The form / genre** – to set it out as a play.
- **The language** – people do not speak in the way poets write so you would have to write the characters' speech realistically, probably including non-standard variations.

The **purpose** (to entertain) and the **audience** may stay the same.

Example 2

If you were adapting a playscript from 1945 to an up-to-date novel you would need to change:

- **The form / genre** – take it out of a script format and put it into the form of a novel.
- **The language** – if one of the characters said, 'I'm feeling jolly spiffing today my man!', you would need to adapt it to something like 'I'm feeling great today, mate!'.

The **purpose** (to entertain) and the **audience** may stay the same. However, you may be asked to write for a different audience and then you would have to adapt the language that you use to suit the audience.

Context

Context

Context is a term used in language science. It is a way of studying language. You need to think about language according to where it is found (i.e. its context).

There are two types of context:
- **Verbal context.**
- **Social context.**

Verbal Context

Verbal context refers to:
- The words that are said.
- Why the words are said.
- Who says the words.
- Who the words are said to.

Verbal context influences the way we understand expressions. Celebrities often say their quotes were taken 'out of context' if they come across as rude or ignorant after an interview. For example, if a celebrity said, 'I hate it when children scream in restaurants', but the interviewer quotes them as saying only, 'I hate children', the words are taken out of context and make the celebrity sound like a bad person.

Similarly, words need to be used in the right context. You might use a swear word in front of a friend, but not in front of a teacher or your parents.

It's important to use the right words for the context you are in. Words must be considered within the rest of the sentence in which they are found.

Social Context

When you consider any text and the way it has been written, or how to respond to it as a reader or listener, you must consider the social context.

Social context refers to:
- Where it takes place – it might be a different country with different customs and conventions to ours.
- When it was written – a particular period in history or in a person's life.
- Its purpose – if you were at a family dinner party and told a very rude joke, it would be inappropriate – the wrong joke for the wrong place!
- Who it is said to – the text must be appropriate for the audience.
- Who said it – the person communicating must use appropriate language – the right words and the right topic. If your science teacher used swear words in class to tell you about her raucous holiday, both the topic and the language would be inappropriate.

It is important to consider social context. For example, if you are studying a novel by Charles Dickens, it would be important to consider:
- The time that it was written.
- The social conventions of that time.
- Social class divisions at that time.
- The way that society worked at that time.
- The way people used language at that time.

If you did not consider these factors, you might interpret things out of context and, therefore, you would not respond in the way that the writer intended.

Traits of Speech

Non-verbal Communication

We communicate with others using speech, but we also communicate through our facial expressions and our body language. These features are known as **non-verbal communication**.

Facial Expressions

Facial expressions reveal our emotions and tell others how we are feeling. Sometimes we have to be careful that we do not give our emotions away through our facial expressions. For example, when your grandmother buys you something for Christmas that you do not like, you have to try to look pleased so that she does not get upset.

Good poker players are said to have a 'poker face'. This refers to a facial expression that does not reveal any emotions (so that the other players cannot tell whether the player has a good hand or not). The term 'poker-faced' is now used to mean straight-faced or serious-faced.

People express their emotions through facial gestures. You can tell when people are happy, sad, confused, etc.

as it shows on their face. Our eyes, foreheads and mouths give away our emotions and our reactions: we cry when we are sad; we smile when we are happy and we frown when we are confused.

Writers can reveal how a character is feeling, or reacting to a situation by describing the character's expressions. For example:

- *'He said, glumly'*, reveals that the character is unhappy.
- *'Her expression was one of sheer delight'*, reveals the character's happiness.
- *'He smiled and reluctantly moved towards the door'*, tells us that although he is smiling, he does not really want to leave.

These are examples of how language can be used for effect. Specific words are chosen to have an impact on the reader.

Note: This comparison of non-verbal communication and how emotion can be shown in writing is an example of how all the parts of the English course, the English Language course and this revision guide are interrelated.

Traits of Speech

Body Language

Body language is the term used to describe our body movements that reveal our emotions. We communicate with our body language; it is another part of non-verbal communication.

For example:
- If you hug yourself, wrapping your arms around your body, you are said to be feeling vulnerable or threatened.
- If you face someone straight on and stand up straight with your chest out, you are considered to be confrontational or even aggressive.

The police study the body language of suspects when they are being interviewed because it can reveal as much about them as the words that they use.

Body signs are interpreted in different ways but here are some commonly believed signs:
- Eyes moving to the right or left – the person is lying.
- Looking you straight in the eye – the person is telling the truth.
- Shoulders slumped – the person is feeling defeated or unconfident.

People can manipulate others by controlling their body language and their facial expressions – note the example of the poker player on page 44.

Sounds not Words

Another feature of non-verbal communication is the sounds that people make that are not words. For example:
- People make a 'huh' sound if they are bored or not happy.
- People sigh if they are bored.
- People laugh if they are happy.

Whilst these sounds are verbal (because they come out of people's mouths), they are not words. However, they can reveal how people are thinking or feeling.

Helpful Hint

Note that some people know how to use their body language. For example, when boxers go into the ring they adopt a confident, aggressive pose, but they are probably feeling apprehensive or even nervous. They just do not want to let their emotions show.

Presenting

Giving Effective Presentations

Before You Begin
- Be sure of your audience – who you are talking to.
- Be sure of your purpose – e.g. to persuade, inform, entertain.

Creating Your Presentation
- Use language that suits the purpose and audience. Use formal language if you are addressing an adult audience; you might use informal and less complicated language if you are addressing younger children.
- Plan what you are going to say very carefully. Research the topic and make notes, then use these notes to write out your speech.
- Use appropriate visual aids, such as pictures, graphs and diagrams.
- Make sure that what you are saying flows and connects together logically (see page 80).
- Use humour, but only if it is appropriate – humour can keep your audience engaged.
- Have a definite, clear opening where you address your audience and make it clear what you are going to talk about. For example:
  - *Good morning Year 11, I am here today to talk to you about the issues of global warming and the things that we can do as a school to try to reduce our carbon footprint...*

Delivering Your Presentation
- Deliver your speech clearly – you need to make sure that you can be heard.
- Use a varied voice pattern – if you sound like a robot, all in the same pitch, you will bore the audience and they will lose interest.
- Use different intonation – your voice should go up and down, and you should give emphasis in the right places.
- If you use a rhetorical question, make it clear by your voice going up at the end of the sentence.
- If you use an exclamation, make sure that your audience can hear it – your voice would go up at the end.
- Use the right tone, e.g. if the subject is sad, make sure that you sound sad.
- Have a memorable ending and make it clear that you are ending your presentation. For example:
  - *Finally, I would like to say...*
  - *To conclude my presentation...*
  - *Thanks for being an attentive audience and for taking the time to listen...*
  - *Does anyone have any questions?*

Additional Tips

- Always prepare your speech well. Research your topic so that you have enough to talk about. Write everything down – even if only in note form so that you do not dry up or run out of things to say.
- Write your speech out in larger font so that you can refer to it easily, and use a highlighter to stress the parts you want to emphasise when speaking.
- Practise first – talk to your mirror!
- Remember to address your audience – make regular eye contact. Do not just read off your script.

Helpful Hint

You could use Microsoft PowerPoint for a presentation or talk. Do not put too much text on your slides; talk about them, rather than reading them.

Discussing and Listening

Taking Part in Discussions and Debates

When there is a discussion or debate taking place, or you are asked to watch a presentation about a topic and then work in a group afterwards to come up with ideas and opinions, you will be assessed on your skills to join in the discussion effectively.

To do this well, you must be able to do the following:

- Listen carefully to what is being said – take brief notes if this helps you remember the ideas and opinions that are expressed.
- Work out if the topic is controversial and is inviting you to agree or disagree with what is being said.
- Form your own opinions on the topic and be ready to put them across when you are given the chance to do so.
- Ask questions to show that you are involved in the topic – but only at appropriate times – and ask for clarification if you are not clear at any point.
- Express your opinions clearly – think about what you want to say and how you are going to express yourself – be careful not just to blurt out things that might not take the discussion forward.
- Ask people for their opinions and listen to what they have to say – do not dismiss other people's opinions off-hand. For example, do not just say, 'I don't agree' or 'That's rubbish'; try saying, *'I've listened to what you have to say, and I can see the point that you're making, but in my opinion… because…'.* Try to back up what you say with facts and ideas.

- Make relevant comments and contributions – they must be related to the topic.
- Do not shout. Try to express yourself calmly, even if you feel strongly about the topic being discussed or the opinions being expressed.

Being a Good Listener

Being a good listener involves certain skills, including:
- Listening to different people's ideas first and then challenging them in the way described opposite.
- Not interrupting people – listen to what people say before responding.
- Allowing everybody to express their ideas and opinions in a group situation. Try to get everyone involved instead of just listening to those with the loudest voices.
- Showing that you can interact with everyone in the group and respond appropriately to each person.

Helpful Hint

Be aware of your body language – if you fold your arms and scowl, it will suggest that you are unwilling to take part and do not agree with anything that is being said. This may be seen as a negative contribution to the discussion or debate.

Remember that non-verbal signs are important – a nod of the head can show someone that you are listening to what they say, and that you might agree with what is being expressed.

Role Play

Role play is when you take on the part of another character and act in role (as if you were that person).

Many students find role play one of the hardest tasks to do, as it is like acting the part. You have to take on the life of another character, and act and react as they would do in the situation that you have been given.

You will probably have already had a go at role play in the course of your studies. Do not worry – you do not have to be a great actor to do well in this task.

Carrying Out Role Play Successfully

To do well in the role play, you must be able to do the following:
- Know the character that you have taken the role of well. You will have done character studies when you studied texts – use these notes to help you to prepare to take on the role. If it is a text that you have studied, you will have explored the character already and will know what they are like.
- Imagine how the character would feel in the given situation, not how *you* would feel, and how *they* would react, not how *you* would react.
- Show that you understand the character by the way that you use speech, gesture and movement.
- Remember to use non-verbal signs. For example, if your character would feel uncomfortable in a situation, try to reflect that in your own body language.

Showing Emotions

If your character is confident, try to reflect that in your voice and the way that you reply. Use confident body language (non-verbal signs), which includes the head being held high, shoulders back, a swaggering walk, standing up straight and looking directly at the audience or the person asking the question.

If your character is timid or uncomfortable, try to reflect that by sounding unsure or nervous in your voice. Use appropriate body language, such as looking down at the ground, hunching your shoulders, shuffling, slouching and not looking directly at the people talking to you.

Speaking slowly and deliberately suggests that a character is thinking about what they are saying – perhaps stressing their points or trying not to make a mistake. If a character is speaking quickly and rambling it shows that they are nervous, lying or very excited.

If there are conflicts between the characters make sure that you show them. For example, if you know that two characters hate each other, show this in your behaviour.

Helpful Hint

Remember to react to situations as the character would – think about how they would react.

Even if you are not the greatest 'actor', if you can respond appropriately as the character (in role) you can do well in this task.

Speeches

There are many techniques used by speech writers to hold the audience's interest and to try to influence their views.

Like any piece of writing, speeches should be organised into clear sections. They should contain language that grabs the audience's attention. However, speeches are written to be read out loud so you need to use language devices that can be heard.

Speeches are often written to persuade. For example, a political speech is written to try to persuade the audience to vote for that party. You may get a question such as this:

Q **Write and deliver a speech where you persuade the audience that free university education should be available to everyone.**

Language Devices for Speeches

- **Use of three** is frequently used in speeches. It may be three questions, three rhetorical questions, three points, etc. Use of three enables you to emphasise a point and is very effective when spoken aloud, e.g. 'I came, I saw, I conquered'.
- **Repetition** emphasises words and phrases and makes them stick in the listener's mind.
- **Parallelism** involves the repetition of sentences with similar structures, e.g. 'It was the best of times; it was the worst of times'.
- **Contrasts and opposites** are used in speeches for emphasis by putting one word or idea next to a different word or idea, e.g. 'Arise fair sun and kill the envious moon'. This contrasts the sun with the moon, and life with death. Opposites work in the same way, e.g. 'It's a matter of life and death'.
- **Rhetorical questions** are effective in speeches as they address the listeners in a way that makes them feel involved.
- **Use of personal pronouns** (I, me, you, he, him, she, her, it, we, us, they, them), possessive pronouns (our, my), and friendly terms of address (e.g. 'Comrades', 'Friends') breaks down barriers between the speaker and the audience, making the audience feel more involved. The use of 'I' also indicates the speaker's authority.
- **Emotive and sensational language** in a speech can make the audience feel a certain way, such as sympathetic or shocked.
- **Lists**: listing subjects, items, names, etc. can emphasise how many/few there are of something, e.g. listing the countries where millions live in poverty highlights the extent of the problem.
- **Exclamatory sentences** (e.g. 'This is unbelievable!') stress a sentence or a point.

Preparation Task

Look at the following part of a speech given by a student to a year 10 assembly. It is about bullying and what to do if you are a victim. Which speech-writing techniques has the student used to engage the audience? Could this speech be improved? Write your own speech for this audience about this topic.

> Good morning year 10. I have been asked to come and talk to you today about a topic that can blight the lives of young people – bullying.
>
> Bullying can take many forms: verbal, physical and mental, and I am sure that at some point you have all felt that you were the victim of at least one of these types of abuse.
>
> Let's look at each one of these forms of bullying and the ways that you can get help if you are targeted by a bully.
>
> Firstly, there is verbal abuse – 'you're fat', 'you're ugly', 'nobody likes you' [pointing at members of the audience at random to get their attention]. How does that make you feel? Many people crumble when they are called names, and I don't believe the old adage, 'Sticks and stones can break your bones but names can never hurt you.' Of course they can! If you get called names you feel terrible, you wonder why you are being picked on and you wonder what you can do to stop it.
>
> The answer is, bullies don't randomly pick their victims; they pick on people who they think will not report their abuse, and those whom they are sure will not get them back.
>
> This is your strength – don't be one of these people! If you get called names or are the victim of verbal abuse – tell someone. Two are stronger than one and the school has a solid anti-bullying policy. The teachers have to take you seriously or they could find themselves in serious trouble...

Practice Questions

Q Write a speech to deliver to your classmates arguing for school uniform to be abolished.

Q Write a speech to deliver to a general audience, persuading them that free university education should be available to everyone.

(See pages 50–51 for more tips on writing and delivering a speech.)

Writing and Delivering a Speech

The following is an example of the type of controlled assessment task you might get for Unit 2:

Q **Write and deliver a persuasive speech to the class about the government ban on smoking in enclosed public spaces. You can be for or against.**

These two pages explain the process you would need to go through to complete this task, along with an example of a finished speech.

You will see again how many of the things that we have covered so far in this revision guide are coming together – speech traits, persuasive language and effective communication.

Think about:
- **Form / genre** – a speech.
- **Language** – think about the register and the style you need to use, based on form, audience and purpose.
  - **Register** (words used) refers to whether you need to use formal or informal language. You could use either here.
  - **Style** is created by your use of many persuasive devices.
- **Audience** – the task states that the audience is your class – teenagers. So perhaps you might use informal language and references that teenagers can relate to.
- **Purpose** – the task states that the purpose is to persuade. You can use the same techniques that are covered on pages 20–21.

Structuring Your Speech

- **Introduction** – make sure that you have a clear introduction that states your case.
- **Main body of the speech** – make your points, one per paragraph, and back them up with evidence, facts and/or your opinion. Highlight any words that you want to stress when you are giving your speech.
- **Conclusion** – always sum up your points and have a definite conclusion that shows the audience that you have finished.

Helpful Hint

Try using visual aids in your speech. For example, you could use a projector to show images of blackened lungs or sad children looking at their parents smoking for a visual impact.

Delivering Your Speech

- Speak clearly and confidently and make sure you keep looking up at your audience, rather than burying your head in your speech!
- Stress certain words (you might have highlighted these when you were writing your speech).
- Pauses get your audience's attention as they wait to see what you are going to say next.
- Remember to vary the tone and pitch of your voice in order to maintain interest.
- Use the correct intonation, for example, your voice will go up when you have a rhetorical question or an exclamatory sentence.

Techniques for Persuasive Speeches

- Use a positive opening sentence to grab the audience's attention.
- Use suitable connectives to connect ideas and give structure and cohesion to the piece (see page 80).
- Use positive or negative vocabulary to influence your audience's opinion.
- Use repetition to emphasise your main points.
- Direct personal address to the audience will make them feel more involved, e.g. using 'you'.
- The present tense will make the issue seem more immediate.
- Personal pronouns, (e.g. 'I', 'you', 'he', 'she', 'they'), give a personal tone to the issue and make the audience feel more involved.
- Using a formal tone will make your opinion seem more credible.
- Rhetorical questions make the audience question the issue.
- Use exclamatory sentences – sentences that end with an exclamation mark, which you stress when you speak.

Helpful Hint

You could also use the techniques covered in persuasive writing. Remember, speeches are written to be delivered to listeners. The techniques used in persuasive writing and speaking will be the same, but with a speech, it is the presentation and delivery that make it effective.

Writing and Delivering a Speech

Here is an example of part of a persuasive speech. The techniques discussed on page 49 are highlighted. (Also look out for some of the persuasive words and phrases discussed on page 32 as writing to persuade uses similar techniques.)

Q **Write and deliver a persuasive speech to the class about the government ban on smoking in enclosed public places. You can be for or against.**

Use of 'I' and present tense makes argument seem believable

Opinion clearly stated

Point
Evidence
Explanation

Giving an alternative view

Connectives used to help structure the argument

Rhetorical questions used to involve the reader

Use of three and rhetorical questions

Discrediting the other opinion

Exclamations are used to emphasise the point

Conclusion summarises opinion

Metaphor to stress the point

Good morning. I am here today to give you my views on whether the government was right to ban smoking in all enclosed public places.

I personally believe that the government's decision to ban smoking in all enclosed public places was the right one. Smoking is an expensive addiction, which is bad for your health. It is thought that smoking is as addictive as some class A drugs, and it has a devastating effect on the health of those who get hooked. Smoking destroys your heart and lungs, makes you look old before your time and will most probably kill you. Three out of five smokers will die from smoking-related illnesses.

The law tries to protect young people from smoking, by making the legal age for buying cigarettes 18. This has been done because the younger a person is when they start smoking, the more likely they are to continue smoking and the harder it is for them to quit. By banning smoking in public places, young people are less likely to see people smoking and be tempted to try it themselves.

The reasons why I support the ban are numerous. Firstly, it is unfair for non-smokers to have to suffer from passive smoking, which itself has health risks associated with it.

Secondly, we all know the risks associated with passive smoking. Roy Castle, a famous musician, never smoked a cigarette in this life, but he died from lung cancer. This, it has been suggested, was the result of working in a smoky atmosphere in the clubs and pubs. Surely smokers do not have the right to inflict their filthy habit on healthy non-smokers?

Thirdly, the ban has made enclosed public places much more pleasant for everyone. Who wants to smell of cigarette smoke whenever they come home from a night out? Who wants to have their air polluted? Who wants to die because of another person's bad habit? Not me!

Some people argue that instead of banning smoking in all public places, we should have followed the example of the Spanish government. In Spain, public bars and restaurants have to clearly state outside whether they allow smoking or not. This means that before entering, the public have a choice – to enter or not. This approach allows both smokers and non-smokers to be happy. But this approach does little to discredit the smokers and discourage people from smoking. In my opinion this is not a good move. I think that we were right in this country to enforce the complete ban.

Finally, I believe that in the long term, the smoking ban is a positive step. The nation's health will improve and fewer young people will start smoking. I fully support the government's decision!

To conclude – smoking ban means smoking beaten! The destructive plague that's been endemic in our society for far too long will hopefully soon be wiped out.

Thanks very much for listening. Does anyone have any questions?

Understanding Creative Texts

Unit 3: Understanding and Producing Creative Texts/ Understanding Spoken and Written Texts and Writing Creatively

Controlled Assessment – Part A: Reading

Unit 3 of both the English specification and the English Language specification requires you to understand and be able to produce creative texts.

Unit 1, Section A of both courses requires you to respond to **non-fiction** texts (texts that have a factual side to them). However, many non-fiction texts contain features of **creative** texts. For example, an autobiography or a travel journal would want to entertain readers as well as inform or persuade them. Such texts are partly informative /persuasive (i.e. non-fiction texts) and partly entertaining (i.e. creative texts).

Writing to entertain (creative texts) can take many forms and, in fact, most texts are entertaining in some way because if they were not, nobody would read them!

Texts that are written purely to entertain and are known as creative texts include:
- Novels and short stories.
- Poems.
- Play scripts and film scripts.
- Some television and radio scripts.
- Jokes.
- Fables, myths and legends.
- The texts in the AQA Anthology.

All of these are creative texts. They are made up by the writer (i.e. they are fictional) and they aim to entertain the reader.

Creative Texts and Creative Writing

You will have studied many creative texts during your English or English Language course. You will be familiar with the writer's techniques for engaging the reader.

You will have studied the following:
- **Characters** – what the characters are like as people and how the writers show this in what they say and do.
- **Settings** – where the action takes place and the writers' descriptions of places.
- **Themes** – the ideas and concepts that the writers want to explore, for example, friendship, hatred, human relationships.
- **Relationships** – between the characters in the texts and links with other texts that you have studied.
- **Style** (language) – the language that the writers use and its effect on the reader.
- **Form and genre** – conventions expected from certain types of writing.

What is the Examiner Looking For?

In your controlled assignments the assessor wants to see that you can do the following:
- Interpret a text, i.e. understand what it is about and what it means to you – the effect that it has on you.
- Engage with (i.e. write about and understand) the writer's ideas and attitudes.
- Use the PEE technique to show that you can respond to the language that the writer uses.
- Analyse (i.e. write about) the writer's use of language (use PEE).
- Understand texts in their social, cultural and historical contexts.
- Compare and contrast texts as necessary.

Helpful Hint

It is important that you know this genre of writing so that you don't make the mistake of recreating this type of writing in Unit 1 Section B of the exam – it is only needed for your controlled assignments.

However, remember that there are other texts such as newspaper articles that can entertain, whilst informing you or even persuading you. You may need to respond to creative text techniques in Unit 1, Section A, as well as using them in your creative writing controlled assignment.

Understanding Creative Texts

Skills Needed for Unit 3 Controlled Assessment

Many of the skills that we have covered so far in this book (particularly in the first chapter) are needed for Unit 3 of the course. The focus of Unit 3 is on literary reading.

Unit 3, Part A: Understanding Creative Texts (Literary Reading) / Extended Reading

You need to show that you can do the following:

- Read and understand texts.
- Engage with the writer's ideas and attitudes.
- Use materials from the text to prove points that you make (use the PEE technique).
- Analyse language and structure.
- Make connections between the texts and their contexts.
- Understand texts in their social, cultural and historical contexts.

Unit 3, Part B: Producing Creative Texts / Creative Writing

You need to show that you can do the following:

- Communicate imaginatively.
- Use and adapt texts for a different purpose and/ or audience.
- Use structured and sequenced sentences.
- Use language, grammar and punctuation to produce cohesive texts.
- Use a variety of sentence structures for clarity, purpose and effect.

For English Language Unit 3, Part C, see pages 82–95.

Important Skills for Unit 3

- Awareness of audience, purpose and form.
- Writing in specific genres (i.e. kinds of writing).
- Organising ideas and information.
- Using a variety of sentence structures.
- Using language for effect.
- Being able to analyse the writer's craft and using the PEE technique.
- Having the ability to compare and contrast texts.
- Being able to write about structure and form/genre.

Preparation for Controlled Assessment

- Learn all the technical language terms from this revision guide and make sure that you can apply them to any type of text that uses these techniques. Remember, all language features can be found in all kinds of texts.
- Ensure that you can use the PEE technique effectively and can apply it to any kind of text.
- Make sure that you know how to write for a specific audience and purpose.
- Make sure that you can use a variety of sentence structures.
- Develop your vocabulary – do not go for the easy word (unless it is specifically needed for your audience or purpose) – try to use interesting words.
- Make sure that you can use a range of punctuation, not just full stops and commas (see pages 75–76).
- Make comparisons between the texts.

Helpful Hint

To do well in this part of the course, all the skills that you have acquired throughout your study of all parts of the course need to be used together.

Themes and Ideas

Literary Reading

For the literary reading controlled assignments you are asked to respond to a text. Your response will be focused around three main areas:

- **Themes and ideas.**
- **Characterisation and voice.**
- **Aspects of genre and form.**

Themes and Ideas

You need to look at the themes and ideas that are in the text.

When you have studied texts in class you will have done work on the themes of the texts. The themes will run through the texts. Some common themes are:

- Love.
- Relationships.
- Betrayal.
- The power of nature.
- Men and women and how they are portrayed.
- Growing up.
- Society in a certain time or country.
- Different phases of life from childhood to old age.
- Deceit and corruption.
- Culture.

You will need to show that you can follow the themes in the text and write about them, referring to specific parts of the text with quotes and language analysis (the PEE technique).

Example Controlled Assessment Task

Here is an example of a controlled assessment task:

Q **Explore the ways relationships are presented.**

The following shows you how you should approach this task.

Introduction – write a paragraph about the title, explaining what you are going to cover in your assignment. For example:

- *Throughout* Wuthering Heights, *a variety of family relationships are presented, none of them in a particularly positive light.*
  I am going to examine the relationships presented through the Earnshaws and the Clintons. The four relationships that I am going to explore are…'

Main body of the assignment – Deal with one relationship at a time. Make your points about the relationships and then prove the points that you make by referring to the novel citing particular events and episodes. Back up these points with quotes from the text. Use PEE.

Conclusion – Sum up the points that you have made in your essay. For example:

- *Therefore, as we can see, the relationships portrayed in* Wuthering Heights *are destructive and, although passion and love are explored, it is their negative sides that seem to dominate the book.*

Helpful Hint

'Explore' means 'write about in detail', referring to the text as much as you can to prove the points that you make. This is where you hit the criteria to be able to use 'supporting textual detail', which gain you marks in the top mark band.

Characterisation and Voice

Characterisation and Voice

You need to look at how characters are presented in texts and how the author's voice is put across, or how the characters are presented by the author.

You will have completed character studies on the main, and maybe the minor, characters in the texts that you have studied in class. You will have decided what type of character each one is and you will have referred to the things that they say and do to help you to reach your decision about the characters.

Example Controlled Assessment Task

Here is an example of a controlled assessment task:

Q Explore the way that the central character is presented and developed.

The following shows you how you should approach this task.

Introduction – write a paragraph about the title, explaining what you are going to cover in your assignment. For example:

- *The main character in* Jane Eyre *is indeed Jane herself. We follow her journey from an unsure, shy orphan to a strong, independent young woman. She grows throughout the novel through each of her experiences. I am going to look at the main events in her life and show what effect they have on her character…*

Main body of the assignment – Deal with one aspect of her character at a time. Make a list of words that you think describe the character and then go on to prove your points.

For a character assignment you could deal with character traits one at a time and show them throughout the text, or deal with events and what they reveal about the character. Decide which you think is the best way for you to do it. Make your points about the character and then prove the points that you make by referring to the novel – particular events and episodes. Back up these points with quotes from the text.

You will need to show that you have understood the character in the text and can write about them, referring to specific parts of the text and using quotes and language analysis (the PEE technique).

Conclusion – Sum up the points that you have made in your essay. For example:

- *To conclude, Jane Eyre transforms from a quiet, unsure little girl into a confident and assured young woman who achieves the happiness that she deserves.*

Here are some useful words to describe characters:

Anxious	Generous	Proud
Apathetic	Ignorant	Reserved
Bold	Jealous	Stubborn
Brave	Loving	Tenacious
Cautious	Masterful	Understanding
Defiant	Nasty	Venerable
Enigmatic	Oppressive	Willing

Helpful Hint

How the character is **presented** refers to how the author portrays them and what they say and do. How are they presented to the reader?

How the character is **developed** refers to how they change or are shown at different places in the text.

Practice Question

Choose one of the texts you have studied in class and write approximately 1600 words in response to:

Q Explore the way that the central character is presented and developed.

Aspects of Genre and Form

Genre

Genre describes the kind of writing that a text belongs to, according to certain features that it has. There are many genres, including:

- Horror.
- Ghost stories.
- Love stories.
- War.
- Comment on society.
- Autobiography.
- Biography.
- Comedy.
- Action/adventure.
- Nature.
- Murder mystery.
- True life stories.

Each genre has certain traits/stylistic features (aspects of form).

For example, a text in the genre of horror will contain gruesome events, death, blood, murder and an evil protagonist (main character). It will have certain stylistic features, such as suspense, an opening that sets the horror scene, innocent victims, and words that reflect the genre, such as 'evil', 'dark', 'shiver', 'creepy' and 'death'.

It may also have a certain structure: the beginning sets the horror scene; the middle describes the gruesome events, and the ending shows that good triumphs over evil. (But note that some texts will break the expected pattern).

Look out for vocabulary, places and characters in the extracts to see to which genre the writing belongs.

Preparation Task

Working with a friend, take one of the texts that you have studied and decide which genre it fits into.

List the features of the genre – the things that you would expect it to have and collect ten quotes from the text that you think reflect the genre.

PEE the quotes, referring to genre. For example:

- *'The monster moved stealthily across the courtyard. She shuddered as its tentacles reached out for her and she let out a blood-curdling scream.'*

  This description contains the diction (words) associated with the horror genre. The 'blood-curdling scream' tells the reader that she is terrified and helps us to feel her fear, engaging us with the horror of the moment.

Aspects of Genre and Form

Form

Form refers to the layout and expectations of the type of text that you are studying. The conventions of the form will decide how it is set out on the page. Different forms include:

* Playscripts.
* Movie scripts.
* Poems.
* Plays.
* Novels.
* Short stories.
* Fables.
* Adverts.

Again, each form will have certain traits and stylistic features. They look different: for example, a play script will have the characters' names down the left-hand side of the page, and their speech will be written out towards the right-hand side of the page; a novel will have the text across the entire page.

Texts in different forms use language associated with the form. For example, novels and poems tend to use a lot of descriptive language. (But note that they may break with the norm, or what we expect of them, in order to create effect).

Example Controlled Assessment Task

Here is an example of a controlled assessment task:

Q **Explore the significance to the whole text of a selected key section.**

In a task like this, you would be given a section of the text that you have been studying. You need to be able to link the passage/section to the rest of the text.

Highlight the passage and make notes at the side, considering:

* Genre and form.
* Character.
* Setting.
* Language use.
* Style.

Preparation Task

Look out for examples where the form is not what you might expect. An example of this might be a poem that is set out as a newspaper report.

Responding to Creative Texts – Checklist

'storm of controversy'
(Metaphor)

Many of the writers' techniques that are covered earlier in this revision guide apply to creative texts because they are all examples of the 'writer's craft' (i.e. the writer's ability to use language to influence the reader).

Here is a reminder of things to look out for when you are reading, and responding to, a creative text.

Accent: the way a character would sound if they were speaking aloud. For example, Cheryl Cole has a Newcastle or 'Geordie' accent, which makes her sound friendly and approachable. People with a non-standard accent were often regarded as less educated in the past, whereas people who used Standard English were regarded as upper class and more educated. This is not thought today but it was in the past.

Adjectives: these are words that describe nouns, e.g. 'great', 'harsh', 'excruciating', 'yellow', 'bright'. Writers use them to paint a picture in the reader's mind.

Adverbs: these are words that describe verbs (the action), e.g. 'carefully', 'quietly', 'quickly'. They can be used to add more detail to an action so that the reader can picture what is going on and how.

Alliteration: repetition of a sound at the beginning of words, e.g. 'Cruel Catherine….'. It is used to stress certain words or phrases to make a point to the reader.

Contrast: a strong difference between two things. A writer might write a paragraph about a beautiful place and follow it with a paragraph describing a run-down place to show the differences between the ways in which two different groups of people live.

Dialect: the words and grammar that speakers use. Regional dialects differ from the Standard English dialect. Each dialect has its own special words and ways of using grammar. A writer might give two characters different dialects to show that they are from different social groups.

Exclamations: show anger, shock, horror, surprise and joy, e.g. 'I won!'. They are used to portray emotions and show how a character reacts or is feeling.

Humour: making a character or situation appear in a funny way can be used to mock the character or the place, or it could show that a character is humorous.

Helpful Hint

Remember, some humour is not obvious. For example, Shakespeare's humour is not always obvious. You need to be aware of what the writer intended, even if it does not make us laugh today.

Imagery (including **similes** and **metaphors**): the words allow readers to create an image in their mind and involve the reader in the moment being described.

Irony and **sarcasm:** the use of words to imply the opposite of their meaning. They can tell us a lot about a character or are used to make fun of people or issues.

Juxtaposition: the positioning of two words, phrases or ideas next to, or near, each other. This highlights a contrast between two words, phrases or ideas, e.g. 'The two friends were known as clever Carole and stupid Steven'.

Metaphor: an image created by referring to something as something else, e.g. 'storm of controversy'.

Negative diction: words that are negative, e.g. 'cruel', 'evil', 'dark'. They give a negative tone and can portray negative feelings towards a character or situation.

Onomatopoeia: words that sound like what they describe, e.g. 'The **clash** of the symbols startled John' – the readers can almost hear the sound for themselves.

Personification: making an object/animal sound like a person, giving it human qualities, e.g. 'the fingers of the tree grabbed at my hair as I passed'.

Positive diction: words that are positive, e.g. 'happy', 'glad', 'joyous'. They give a positive tone or portray positive feelings towards a character or situation.

Puns/play on words: words used in an amusing way, e.g. 'She's parking mad!'. Puns entertain and amuse readers, and imply another meaning.

Questions (interrogatives): they show that the writer wants the reader to consider the question, or that they themselves are considering the question. Questions can show a lot about a character and how they are feeling, e.g. upset, confusion.

Received Pronunciation: the accent used by many national newsreaders. You cannot tell which part of the country a Received Pronunciation speaker comes from. This accent is seen as prestigious (impressive) and is often associated with well-educated and wealthy people.

Repetition: when words, phrases, sentences or structures are repeated, which stress certain words or key points in the piece of writing.

Rhetorical questions: questions that do not need an answer. A writer might state, 'Why would he behave that way?'. The writer is asking the reader to consider the question.

Simile: a comparison of one thing to another that includes the words 'as' or 'like', e.g. 'Her voice cut through him like a knife'. This shows how the words upset the character.

Standard English: the conventional use of words and grammar in the English language.

Slang: a non-standard use of words. Teenagers use a lot of slang words when they talk to each other, according to language research, e.g. 'dosh' for money.

Tone: the overall attitude of the writing, e.g. formal, informal, playful, angry, suspicious, ironic. Tone can be used to allow the emotions of the author, or the character, to be expressed.

The PEE Technique

The PEE technique enables you to quote a phrase from the text and then comment upon it. For example:
P (point) 'The writer uses the metaphor…'
E (evidence) 'The skin cracks'.
E (explanation) This describes how dry the land is. The writer compares land to human skin to make the image more vivid for the reader and to enable them to picture the fragility and dryness of the land.

Helpful Hint

Remember, it is not enough to be able to spot the use of these techniques. You must be able to say why the writer has used them and the effect that they have on the reader.

Applying the Creative Texts Checklist

You will be asked to respond to creative texts for your controlled assignment pieces. The checklists that you have covered so far in this revision guide will help you.

Here is an example of a creative text. It is an extract from the novel, *Oliver Twist* by Charles Dickens. You could get a question such as:

Q **How does Dickens show the conditions of the workhouse in this extract?**

The extract has been highlighted and a commentary has been written about it (see page 61). You can follow this example to analyse any text.

- Highlight the text for interesting language features.
- PEE the features that you find.
- Consider the whole text: characters, setting, themes, relationships, historical and cultural points or relevance.

The words that the writer has used, which stand out to the reader, have been highlighted.

For a controlled assignment you might be asked to compare two places or characters that are shown in two different novels. You could be asked to write about how the writer uses language to convey (show) the scenes or characters. You would need to respond to each text, and then compare and contrast the two, drawing out similarities and differences.

The skills covered on this page are needed for both the controlled assessment tasks and the written exam text analysis.

Helpful Hint

It is necessary to read a text at least twice before you see the features. The first time you read it you will understand the content. The second (or third) time you read it, you will see the features that the writer has used in the passage to have a particular effect on the reader.

Extract from *Oliver Twist* by Charles Dickens

The room in which the boys were fed was a large stone hall, with a copper at one end; out of which the master, dressed in an apron for the purpose, and assisted by one or two women, ladled the gruel at mealtimes. Of this festive composition the boys had one porringer and no more - except on occasions of public rejoicing when he had two ounces and a quarter of bread besides. The bowls never wanted washing. The boys polished them with their spoons till they shone again; and when they had performed this operation (which never took very long, the spoons being nearly as large as the bowls), they would sit staring at the copper, with such eager eyes, as if they could have devoured the very bricks of which it was composed; employing themselves meanwhile, in sucking their fingers most assiduously, with the view of catching up any stray splashes of gruel that might have been cast thereon. Boys have generally excellent appetites. Oliver Twist and his companions suffered the tortures of slow starvation for three months. At last they got so voracious and wild with hunger, that one boy who was tall for his age, hinted darkly to his companions that unless he had another basin of gruel, he was afraid he might some night happen to eat the boy sleeping next to him, who happened to be a weakly youth of tender age. He had a wild, hungry eye and they implicitly believed him. A council was held; lots were cast for who should walk up to the master after supper that evening and ask for more; and it fell to Oliver Twist.

Example Response

Here is an example of part of a student's response to the question on the previous page relating to the *Oliver Twist* extract.

The passage describes a meal time in the orphanage, where Oliver Twist spent his early days. Dickens uses language cleverly to show the reader that the boys were near starvation and living in horrible conditions.

We are all familiar with the section of the film or the book when Oliver Twist asks for more please, sir.

In the opening of the passage we are told that the boys 'were fed'. This phrase makes them sound like animals as it is the way that you would refer to animals eating, rather than human beings. This shows the reader that the boys are regarded as little more than animals and not as boys.

The imagery of the boys as animals continues throughout the passage with the phrases, 'wild with hunger', 'wild, hungry eye' and the reference to carnivorous behaviour, 'eating the boy next to him'. These descriptions create images of the boys as wild animals, starving and predatory.

The servers of the food 'ladled the gruel' which creates an image of the lumpy, horrible food that the boys had to eat. It had to be served up with spoons and 'ladled' out.

Dickens states, somewhat ironically, that the 'bowls never wanted washing.' There is dark humour present here. The phrase stresses the fact that the boys licked their bowls clean, and bearing in mind that the food was not very appetising, this shows how hungry they were.

We are told that the operation of eating their food never took very long, 'The spoon being nearly as large as the bowls.'

This stresses the fact that the bowls were tiny and the boys were not given much food.

Alliteration is used in the passage to highlight the sorry situation that the boys are in. They 'sit staring' with 'eager eyes'. The alliteration stresses their pitiful state, as they try to mop up any 'stray splashes' of food from their bowls.

The words help to stress the boys' plight.

Negative diction is also used to stress the horrific situation that the boys find themselves in at this time. We are told that they have, 'Suffered the tortures of slow starvation for three months'. Again, alliteration is used to stress the words that can affect the reader and make them feel great sympathy for the boys.

The negative diction runs throughout the rest of the passage with, 'wild with hunger', 'hinted darkly', 'wild, hungry eye.'

However, there is a touch of humour here too, with the boy suggesting that he was so hungry he might eat the boy next to him!

This is not funny in reality, but the humour helps to highlight the sadness of the situation, especially as the other boys 'implicitly believed him'. The adverb 'implicitly' stresses that they did actually think that he might, so hungry were they all.

Note that:
- PEE has been applied to the highlighted parts of the passage.
- The student has worked their way through the text in the order that it appears. However, if one style feature is noticed and it occurs more than once in the passage, it is dealt with altogether rather than keep repeating the same point. This approach should be applied to any text that you have to analyse.

This response would be awarded the top marks of the mark scheme.

Helpful Hint

Look out for texts that were written in the past – the language used in them and the situations in them may differ from what we are used to today.

You need to be aware of a text's historical context in order to respond to it appropriately.

Responding to Characters

Characters in texts are presented in a variety of ways. The techniques used to present characters will depend on the form/genre of the text to which you are responding.

You get to understand the characters through what they say and do. The writer portrays them, using language, in a carefully chosen way so that the reader thinks about the characters in the way that the writer wants them to.

Characters in Novels and Short Stories

In novels and short stories, characters are portrayed through:
- Their actions – what they say and do.
- The way that they react, and interact, with other people.
- The way that they respond to situations.
- How they develop or change in the course of the text.
- What they say and how they say it. For example:
  - *He replied sarcastically, 'I really don't think so.'*
    This sentence tells us about the character through the adverb, which describes how he speaks. Adverbs tell us a lot about characters so pay particular attention to them.

Characters in Dramatic Monologues (Heard)

In dramatic monologues, the focus is on one character. The audience only sees or hears their viewpoint and their view of things. But you can read between the lines to find out more than the character reveals.

The audience responds directly to the character through what the character tells them and how they tell it.

In dramatic monologues, the character is portrayed through:
- What they say and how they say it.
- What they choose to tell the audience about.
- The events that they talk about.
- The opinions that they share with the audience.
- The views that they express about things.
- Their tone of voice.
- Their use of accent and dialect.
- Sound effects.
- Their stress, intonation and pauses.

Characters in Dramatic Monologues (Performed)

In dramatic monologues that are performed, the character is portrayed through the same techniques as in dramatic monologues that are meant to be heard, as well as:
- Facial expressions (non-verbal communication signs).
- Body language.
- Movement on the stage.
- Lighting.
- Scene and setting.
- The clothes that a character wears.

Characters in Play Scripts and Film Scripts

Play scripts and film scripts can be set out differently but they share common traits. When you read a script you have to remember that it was written to be performed/seen/heard. This means that it shares elements of all the texts that we have looked at here. It will be different on the page to the way that it is on the screen or the stage.

A director, or a producer, will have interpreted the script in the way they want the audience to see it. The audience responds more to the visual elements in these texts, such as:
- Lighting and sound.
- Camera angles.
- Shot typesetting.
- Sound effects, e.g. music, etc.
- Colour.

Moving Images – Film and Television Texts

During your course you will get the chance to study moving images. Moving images include films, a certain genre of television or maybe even advertisements.

Your Media Literacy will be tested. You will experience, analyse, and maybe even make, media products such as your own short film in a certain genre or a television advert for a product.

Just as when you respond to any text you need to be able to:

- Recognise and comment on the genre (horror film, love story, advert, etc.).
- Use technical terminology that applies to the genre in your analysis.
- Use the PEE technique to enable you to comment on techniques that are used and their effect on the viewer/audience.

You will still use the FLAP technique, but when you look at the style and language, there will be stylistic features that would not apply to written texts.

However, you need to remember that the film or advert will have been written as a script first, so all your skills are being tested.

Some of the terms that you would apply to a moving image text can be seen below.

Media/Moving Images Terms

Genre – the kind of text/media that it is, e.g. a horror film, a cowboy film, a ghost drama.

Conventions – the conventions of a text are the things that you would expect them to have. For example, a horror film will have blood and guts and gruesome events; a ghost drama will have spooky music and lots of dark shots.

Significant use of signs and symbols – the signifier and what is being signified. For example, if a cross is used, the signifier is the cross whereas what is being signified is God or religion.

Media and Moving Images

Camera Shots

Pan – the camera is on some form of tripod and can move from side to side.

Tilt – the camera is moving up and down.

Track – the camera is placed on tracks to enable it to follow someone walking / a car moving, etc.

Crane – the camera is placed on a crane so that it can move up and get high up shots.

Aerial – the camera is placed on a helicopter or small plane to produce an overhead shot or a landscape.

Zoom – the camera goes from a long shot to a close up (zoom in) or vice versa (zoom out).

Arc – The camera moves around in a circular movement whilst the object it is focusing on remains still.

The fade – where the camera fades out, obscuring the thing that it was focusing on.

Sound Effects

Silence and suspense – silence used to build suspense that can be broken by the interruption of noise.

Diegetic sound – the source of the sound is visible. For example, a man playing a piano or a character talking.

Non-diegetic sound – the source of the noise cannot be seen on the screen. For example, a narrator's voiceover, mood music or sound used for a dramatic effect.

Voiceover – a voice talking over the action, rather than the actors delivering the lines live.

Lighting and colour – used to create an effect, usually in keeping with the genre.

Settings – look at the surroundings and how they are portrayed.

Mise-en-scène – the design aspects of a production and what has been put in the scene. Mise-en-scène refers to all of the above.

Responding to Texts

In your controlled assignments you need to show that you can:

- Engage with the writer's ideas and attitudes.
- Interpret how they write, and understand the messages that the writer is trying to put across.
- Make connections between texts if you are asked to compare them.
- Write about the characters, referring to the text in detail.
- Use the PEE technique to prove points.
- Understand texts in their social, cultural and historical contexts.

Example Controlled Assessment Task

The following are two examples of controlled assessment tasks.

Q Explore the way the central character is presented in two of the texts that you have studied. Look at the main character in each text.

Q Compare the way that Macbeth is presented in *Macbeth* when he is first introduced to the audience, with the way that Atticus is portrayed in *To Kill A Mockingbird*.

As we saw previously, different forms/genres (e.g. a play and a novel, as in the task above) will use different techniques to portray their characters.

These tasks are asking for your response to the characters, but also the response that you think the writer wants for the characters:

- **'Explore'** – this is asking you to 'show throughout the text'.
- **'Presented'** – this is asking you how the characters are shown to the audience through the words that the writer uses.

If you are looking at a performance of a play, rather than the play script on paper, the director or producer, as well as the script writer, will have put their interpretations in too.

Template for this Type of Assessment

The following shows you how you should approach task 2.

Introduction – Interpret the question and say in your own words what you are going to do. For example:

- *Macbeth is portrayed as a brave, noble and loyal soldier when he is introduced to the audience. The audience hears about his brave exploits and his loyalty to the king before they meet him.*

Atticus is seen as a humble, well-respected man, who is deeply respected by his children and his community. Here, the two are similar as they are seen through other people's eyes before we see them in action...

Main body of the assignment – write about each character – one point per paragraph is a good model. For each paragraph make a point about their character and use a quote to back up the point that you make. Make comparisons about the characters or refer to similarities as they occur.

Conclusion – show that you have answered the question that you have been asked to explore. For example:

- *Therefore, as we can see, both characters are seen in positive lights at the beginning of the texts. However, although Atticus remains a fine and noble man, Macbeth changes beyond recognition from a brave and loyal soldier to a mad butcher. Atticus ends as he began – a man who deserves our respect.*

Helpful Hint

When you are looking at more than one text, you might be expected to make comparisons and comment on the similarities and differences that exist.

Types of Creative Texts

Film Scripts

Film scripts are written in order to tell everyone making the film what it is about and how the actors should deliver their words and actions. The film script is a document that is translatable to film.

A certain type of layout (form) is used for writing scripts. This correct script layout makes it easier for everyone who must read the screenplay – script assessors, investors, directors, producers, crew, cast, editors, sound mixers, etc. – so that even if they are scanning it in the back seat of a car at 2am on the way to the location, it is immediately obvious what is going on, who is saying what, what the point of the scene is, and the subtext.

The following list describes features that are all evident in the film script below. Remember them when responding to texts and writing your own pieces.

- Directions in the present tense.
- Described so that a producer can make the shots.
- No need for speech marks in a script.
- Not too much descriptive language.
- The speech should try to sound like how a real person would really speak.

Preparation Task

Find the features mentioned above in the film script below.

Example of a Film Script

THE GONE AND THE FORGOTTEN

EXTERNAL SHOT. FLAT. DAY

FADE UP on an open window of a block of flats on the second floor.

The sound of a rugby match on TV is blaring through the open window.

INTERNAL SHOT. FLAT - LIVING ROOM. DAY.

The television screen shows a rugby game but Andy, a man of about thirty, is ignoring it completely.

He is standing next to the mantlepiece over the fire, looking at a photo. It is a photo of him and Karen at a theatre restaurant, taken five years earlier.

ANDY OFF SCREEN

Aren't we happy the way we are?

INTERNAL SHOT. FLAT - KITCHEN. DAY

Andy takes a can of beer from the fridge and rips it open. He lifts it to his mouth and takes a large swig.

Andy goes over to the blender on the bench. He turns it upside down. There is an inscription on it: "Love to Karen on her twenty-eighth birthday. Andy."

Andy presses the cover on the blender causing it to whirl violently into life. Andy leaps back from it, and the blender stops as suddenly as it started.

Page 117

Types of Creative Texts

Speeches

Speeches can fit into both categories of writing – they use creative techniques, but are also examples of non-fiction writing, as they deal with facts.

There are a number of language techniques that are often applied to speeches, such as use of three and rhetorical questions.

The following list describes features that are all evident in the speech below. Remember them when responding to texts and writing your own pieces.

- Formal language is used as the speech is addressing a huge audience.
- Repetition is used.
- Serious tone.
- Negative diction.
- Positive diction for what could be achieved.
- Mixture of facts, emotions and opinion.
- Use of three.
- Rhetorical questions.

Preparation Task

Find the features mentioned above in the speech below.

Example of a Speech

Today there is talk of war everywhere. Everyone fears a war breaking out between the two countries. If that happens it will be a calamity both for India and for Pakistan... I would take leave to say that their argument does not appeal to me. You may ask if I approve of the Union Government approaching the UNO I may say that I both approve and do not approve of what they did. I approve of it, because after all what else are they to do? They are convinced that what they are doing is right. If there are raids from outside the frontier of Kashmir, the obvious conclusion is that it must be with the connivance of Pakistan. Pakistan can deny it. But the denial does not settle the matter. Kashmir has acceded the accession upon certain conditions. If Pakistan harasses Kashmir and if Sheikh Abdullah who is the leader of Kashmir asks the Indian Union for help, the latter is bound to send help. Such help therefore was sent to Kashmir. At the same time Pakistan is being requested to get out of Kashmir and to arrive at a settlement with India over the question through bilateral negotiations. If no settlement can be reached in this way then a war is inevitable... Is this what is wanted? Is this what is needed? Will this stop the bloodshed?
I shall therefore suggest that it is now their duty, as far as possible, to arrive at an amicable understanding with India and live in harmony with her. Mistakes were made on both sides. Of this have no doubt. But this does not mean that we should persist in those mistakes, for then in the end we shall only destroy ourselves in a war and the whole of the sub-continent will pass into the hands of some third power. That will be the worst imaginable fate for us. I shudder to think of it. Therefore the two Dominions should come together with God as witness and find a settlement...

Mahatma Gandhi

Types of Creative Texts

Play Scripts

Play scripts are an example of a type of creative text that is written to be spoken and performed (and, therefore, watched or listened to by an audience).

Play scripts have features of both spoken and written language. They need to provide the actors and the director with the information they need in order to stage and perform the play.

The following list describes features that are all evident in the play script below. Remember them when responding to texts and writing your own pieces.

- Details of act and scene.
- Stage directions for the actors.
- Brackets describing how the words should be performed.
- Short sentences, as used in everyday speech.
- Archaic language – it sounds old, not like the way we would speak today.
- Exclamatory sentences.
- Pauses.
- Fillers.
- Repetition.

Preparation Task

Find the features mentioned above in the play script below.

Example of a Play Script

```
Macberry the Play (based on Macbeth)


ACT II SCENE I: Outside Macberry's castle. It is a cold
and dark night, the wind is howling through the trees.


Enter Banktop, and Fleapit bearing a candle before him.


BANKTOP                  Are you alright, boy?
FLEAPIT (angrily)        Erm, the moon is down; I have
                         not heard the clock.
BANKTOP (confidently)    And she goes down at twelve.
FLEAPIT                  It is later, you silly
                         man!(walking around agitatedly)
                         There's something funny going
                         on. Mark my words, you scoundrel!
BANKTOP                  What do you mean, you, you...
                         demon!
FLEAPIT                  I mean that YOU were never
                         to be trusted.
BANKTOP (pausing)        ME! ME never to be trusted?
```

Types of Creative Texts

Short Stories / Descriptive Writing

Short story writing and creative descriptive writing are **imaginative**.

Example of Descriptive Writing

It seems like I've been having the dreams since before I could possibly dream. I can just imagine it now, a little me inside my mother's stomach, dreaming the dreams that now seem to haunt the living daylights out of me repetitively.

They're almost all pictures and images, fragments of bigger scenes that I look down upon like a weird out-of-body experience. It was like a film, starring me, terrified of my own dreams while I actually watch them.

In the dream there was always a house, or mansion as I liked to call it. It looked like a mansion from Steven King's Rose Red. *It was just smaller and even though it looked lively, it had a sense of sorrow to it that showed in the very gothic-like walls and arches and window panes. As if the house itself was weeping.*

The following list describes features that are all evident in the piece of descriptive writing above. Remember them when responding to texts and writing your own pieces.
- Correct use of commas.
- Paragraphs to structure the writing.
- Coherence and links between the paragraphs.
- Personification.
- Accurate spelling.
- Interesting use of vocabulary that reminds the reader of the horror genre.
- Use of adjectives and adverbs.
- Longer sentences.
- Imaginative, not fact.

Preparation Task

Find the features mentioned above in the descriptive piece of writing.

Poetry

Poetry is another example of creative and descriptive writing.

Example of a Poem

To Autumn, by John Keats

Season of mists and mellow fruitfulness!
*   Close bosom-friend of the maturing sun;*
Conspiring with him how to load and bless
*   With fruit the vines that round the thatch-eaves run;*
To bend with apples the mossed cottage trees,
*   And fill all fruit with ripeness to the core;*
*   To swell the gourd, and plump the hazel shells*
With a sweet kernel; to set budding more,
*   And still more, later flowers for the bees,*
*   Until they think warm days will never cease,*
*   For Summer has o'erbrimmed their clammy cells.*

The following list describes features that are all evident in the poem above. Remember them when responding to texts or writing your own pieces.
- Alliteration.
- Exclamatory sentence.
- Personification.
- Positive diction.
- Verbs that suggest plenty and fullness.
- Reliance on adjectives to create images for the reader.

Preparation Task

Find the features mentioned above in the poem.

Helpful Hint

You should notice that the creative writing examples have more of the stylistic features found on pages 58–59. The writers have used a host of creative techniques to have a particular impact on the reader.

Creative Non-fiction Texts – Examples

The following are examples of non-fiction texts. They deal with facts and real topics. However, as you can see, they contain stylistic features which are found in creative texts to make them readable and interesting.

When studying or writing your own texts, always remember to consider FLAP:

- Form
- Language
- Audience
- Purpose.

Example 1

Form – Film review on a website.
Language – See highlighted features.
Audience – General adults, people interested in films.
Primary purpose – To inform and entertain.

- Pun in the headline
- Exclamatory sentence
- Informal language/Informal register
- Use of adjectives
- Simile
- Colloquial, chatty tone

Nicolas Cage Will Drive Angry
It's a car chase revenge flick – in 3D!
Source: The Hollywood Reporter

Just when you thought 3D couldn't get any more terrifying – here comes Nic Cage.

The Oscar-winning star's bulging eyes and idiosyncratic hairline will be comin' atcha like Cleopatra in the wonderfully-named revenge thriller, *Drive Angry*.

The title pretty much tells you all you need to know – Cage will play a vengeful father who becomes embroiled in a bloody and protracted car chase with the goons who killed his daughter and kidnapped her baby (so Cage is now playing grandfathers? God, that makes us feel old).

As the miles tick away, the bodies begin to pile up like the points on David Bentley's licence as Cage DRIVES ANGRY.

Sounds pretty simple, and vaguely similar to *Stopping Power*, the ill-fated Jan de Bont/John Cusack thriller, but this seems like a deliberate throwback to the great car chase movies of the 70s and 80s; a blood-soaked *Smokey & The Bandit*, a gore-flecked *Gone In 60 Seconds*, a really *Dirty Mary Crazy Larry*.

Example 2

Form – Documentary script
Language – See highlighted features.
Audience – General
Primary purpose – To inform and persuade.

- Time of filming noted on left-hand side
- Brackets show actions or explain how to say the words in the script
- Speaker's name
- Contractions used to show natural speech

02:08:23:00   INTERVIEWER: Why has the crowd gathered here today, Sally?
(ZOOM IN ON SALLY'S CONCERNED FACE)
SALLY: Well, John... we are sick of the way that schools in Twixham keep closing their Sixth forms. Many students don't want to go to college. They want to stay on in schools that they know and in which they've been successful.
(CHEERS IN THE BACKGROUND FROM THE CROWD)
INTERVIEWER: Many can sympathises with your plight and that of all those around us. (Hand sweeping round the crowd and camera to pan in on faces). However, the Local Council says that it's uneconomical for the schools to have sixth forms, especially those with smaller sixth forms of fewer than 100 students.
SALLY: This might be the case, but you can't really put an economic cost on someone's happiness can you?
(CHEERS FROM THE CROWD)
INTERVIEWER: Ok let's see what some of the crowd have to say on this issue.
(YOUNG MAN WAVING THE INTERVIEWER OVER)
INTERVIEWER: Hello, I can see you have something to say on this issue. What would you like the viewers to know?
INTERVIEWEE: Well, I think that many young people will stop staying on in further education if this is introduced as they simply wouldn't want to attend the local college that has a bad reputation.

Creative Non-fiction Texts – Examples

Example 3

Form – Book review in a newspaper / on a website.
Language – See highlighted features.
Audience – Adults, people who enjoy reading.
Purpose – To inform and entertain.

- Informative tone and formal language
- Fact
- Clear layout with paragraphs
- Adjectives
- Use of compound sentences

The Dogs and the Wolves by Irène Némirovsky, translated by Sandra Smith
The Times Review by Ruth Scurr

The world has been rediscovering Irène Némirovsky since the publication of her unfinished masterpiece, Suite Française, in the original French, and in English translation, in 2004. During her lifetime Némirovsky was a bestselling author and she intended Suite Française as her War and Peace.

Famously, the manuscript was hidden and saved by her daughters after her deportation from Vichy France. After the phenomenal international success of Suite Française, some of Némirovsky's earlier novels and stories have been republished and translated, each contributing something new to our understanding of a writer almost lost from literary history after her death in Auschwitz in August 1942, aged 39.

Sandra Smith's most recent translation, The Dogs and the Wolves, will complicate an uncomfortable debate: was Némirovsky an anti-Semitic Jew? This is not a new question. It was raised in the French introduction to Suite Française (but not in the English introduction). The 2007 translation of David Golder drew more attention to her criticisms of the Jewish milieu to which she belonged (Némirovsky was the daughter of a Jewish banker who fled the Russian Revolution and remade his fortune in France).

Example 4

Form – Website article.
Language – See highlighted features.
Audience – Teenagers, people interested in sports / ping-pong.
Purpose – To inform, persuade and entertain.

- Colloquial / informal language
- Clear layout using paragraphs
- Fact
- Opinion
- Subject-specific jargon
- Use of personal pronoun 'you' throughout
- Directive

Ping Pong
Rate this article: ☆☆☆☆☆
<< Previous article
Next article >>

Ping-pong is a sport that has the reputation for being nerdy and pointless, but if that's your impression of it, you have a lot to learn. Let me explain.

Playing a match is like taking a test: you have to calculate angles and probabilities under time pressure. If you don't determine the right force and acceleration, you might completely miss the ball. Professional table tennis players do not become great overnight, as with any sport. Instead, they dedicate long hours (perhaps spent more productively elsewhere) learning.

It's inevitable: the more you play, the more types of players you'll encounter. The Ping-Pong Dork is the worst kind of challenger. He brings his own signature paddle to the match, insists on using his regulation-standardized ball, will argue for hours about 40 mm versus 38 mm, and actually knows the names of the greatest players in the world. The most pathetic part is he's beaten mercilessly every time.

Then there are the cautious folk, the fear of defeat causing them to play conservatively. A more liberal style, on the other hand, suggests control. You won't try to slam when the game is moving at a fast pace, and you won't attempt a cut serve when the score is 19-20. But when you can exploit the other player's weakness and jump ahead, you're free to miss all the slices and smashes you want.

Don't think for a second this game isn't cutthroat. Ping-pong teaches character. You can win, even if you're down by 10, if you persevere with tenacity. You learn to work against anxiety, sometimes caused by the other player's trick shots, sometimes by spectators, and sometimes by your own psyched-out self.

Creative Non-fiction Texts – Examples

Example 5

Form – Company website homepage.
Language – See highlighted features.
Audience – Adults, existing and potential clients.
Purpose – To inform and persuade.

> Different font sizes

> Menu

> Use of colour

> Highlighted information

> Links

> Technical/industry specific jargon

> Photos

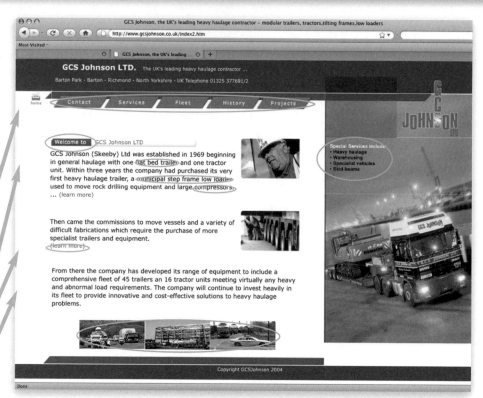

Example 6

Form – Informal letter.
Language – See highlighted features.
Audience – The letter writer's friend, Shabnam.
Purpose – To inform and entertain.

> Informal tone

> Contractions help to create an informal tone

> Non-standard English dialect and colloquial language

> Clear layout in paragraphs

> Familiarity helps to create informal tone

> Exclamatory sentences

Dear Shabnam

You won't believe what a fantastic holiday we had. I had to write to tell you all about it and to make you really jealous! It would have been great if you could have come with us, but I know that wasn't possible this year. Let's make a date to do it for our 18th birthdays.

You know I really wasn't looking forward to going to Florida, as I thought it would be all Disney and noise, but it was amazing! It totally surpassed my expectations. Also, me and my brother only had one argument, which is a miracle for us!

The best part of the holiday was when we went into the everglades on a little boat and saw the most amazing scenery. It was like a desert that had been covered with water, and you could see for miles. We even managed to see some alligators – but luckily from a distance! But it got a bit gross when we went into one of the nearby towns and saw alligator bags and shoes for sale – that did freak me out a bit and you would have hated it! My mum wanted to buy one for gran – she said gran would love one, but I managed to talk her out of it!

Anyway, I'll see you soon.

Sara

Helpful Hint

Whilst an informal letter like the one above can be laid out in any way, a **formal** letter must have the writer's address in the top right corner; the recipient's name and address below it on the left, and the date under the recipient's address.

If you write 'Dear Sir/Madam', sign off with 'Yours faithfully'. If you write, for example, 'Dear Mr Jones', sign off with 'Yours sincerely'.

Producing Creative Texts

Unit 3: Understanding and Producing Creative Texts/ Understanding Spoken and Written Texts and Writing Creatively

Controlled Assessment – Part B: Writing

Remember that you have the option of resubmitting your controlled assignments once in order to achieve better marks.

This page has tips and advice about improving your own creative texts once you have written them.

For Part B of Unit 3 you will have to produce writing in the form of:

- **Recreations** (taking a text and turning it into another).
- **Moving images** (writing based on moving images).
- **Commissions** (responding to a given brief).

Check out the AQA website for examples of these kinds of assessment tasks.

The tasks will predominantly expect you to write in the non-fiction genres that have been covered already in this guide. However, there will always be one recreative task that allows you to produce a narrative.

The tasks are designed to see that you can write for a particular audience and purpose and in a chosen genre.

Some of the tasks will encourage you to produce multi-modal texts in which you combine written language with audio/visual devices. For example, a web page, a film script, a radio script, a radio play or a script for a television advert.

You will need to use the language techniques that apply to responding to non-fiction texts, and you will also need to use the skills that writers of creative texts use.

You must be aware of the style of writing that you use, use appropriate language for the task, and aim the piece at the right audience.

Helpful Hint

Remember that you can resit (once) any units that you are not happy with, so keep persevering and get yourself the best grade that you possibly can.

Ten Tips to Achieve a Grade C or Above in the Writing Tasks

If you need to resubmit a piece of controlled assessment because you did not get the grade that you think you are capable of achieving, it is worth applying the following checklist to your work.

1. Adapt the form/genre and style to meet the needs of the audience and purpose that were specified in the task. Ensure that you use the conventions expected of the genre.

2. Use a range of sentence structures, and vary the length of your sentences and the way in which you start them.

3. Use varied vocabulary to interest the reader and get them involved. For example:
   - 'glorious' instead of 'nice'
   - 'horrific' instead of 'bad'
   - 'stuttered' instead of 'said'
   - 'ambled' instead of 'walked'

4. Do not use the same word repeatedly, especially 'then'. Replace 'then' with adverbs to start sentences. For example:
   - *Then, she decided to go home.*
   - ***Reluctantly**, she decided to go home.*

   The adverb 'reluctantly' shows the reader *how* she did it and gives us an insight into the character. Using 'then' does not tell us any of this.

5. Use adverbs to make sentences more interesting. For example:
   - *She walked towards the opening.*
   - *She walked **cautiously** towards the opening.*

6. Use paragraphs accurately. Roughly, there should be a new paragraph every 8 lines or so. This is not a rule, only a device to help you check that you have used paragraphs correctly.

7. Use punctuation accurately, including full stops, commas, exclamation marks, question marks, colons and semi-colons, brackets and apostrophes.

8. Make sure your spelling is accurate.

9. Use connectives other than 'and' and 'but'. For example, 'although', 'however', 'unless', 'until' (see page 80).

10. Have a good structure – create an interesting opening and a clever ending.

Writing a Creative Non-fiction Text

Always remember, when producing a piece of writing, the writer has to consider the following:

- **Purpose** – why am I writing this piece?
- **Audience** – who am I writing this piece for?
- **Language** – what sort of language (style and tone) should I use? Formal or informal? Simple or technical?
- **Form and genre** – where is the piece of writing going to appear? In a magazine or newspaper? On the Internet? In an advert or leaflet?

When writing your own pieces in the controlled assessment, there are a number of forms you may be asked to write. Each will require different language techniques. Writing leaflets is covered on page 34 and writing speeches is covered on pages 49–50. Writing in other forms, such as play scripts are covered on pages 66–69 and 70–72.

This page describes how to produce a good article for a magazine, newspaper or web page.

Writing Articles

Follow the guidelines below to write an article.

1 Decide what your article will be about.

2 Research the topic and find information about it.

3 In the first paragraph / the first few sentences, make sure you consider:
- Who?
- What?
- When?
- Where?
- Why?

4 Grab the reader's attention by using an interesting headline.

5 Involve and captivate the reader by creating an opening sentence that is a question or something unexpected.

6 Now, give the details. It is always a good idea to include one or two quotes from people involved. Write in the third person (i.e. use 'he', 'she', 'it' or 'they'). Be objective. Use active verbs so the reader feels things are really happening.

7 Use the last paragraph to summarise your article. Try ending with a quote or a catchy phrase.

8 Add a by-line: at the end of your article, state who wrote the article – 'By ….'.

9 Decide where appropriate illustrations / pictures will be placed.

10 Proof-read your article and edit it where necessary.

Preparation Task

Cut out three articles from a newspaper and apply the checklist above – have the writers followed the tips? What other features can you see that are common to these articles?

Common Errors in Writing

Punctuation and Grammar

Punctuation and grammar are very important in order to convey meaning through a piece of writing. You will be expected to use punctuation and grammar correctly in your controlled assessment tasks and in the exam. The following information is provided to help you when you are writing. Read the information through and make sure you understand it.

Full Stops (.)

Full stops separate sentences. Without them, writing does not make sense!

Commas (,)

Commas are used to mark smaller breaks or pauses than full stops. They must not be used to link two separate statements which could stand alone as sentences, unless a connective (e.g. 'and' or 'because' (see page 80) or a word like 'who', 'which' or 'that' is used, for example:
- I fed the dog, which was hungry.   ✓
- I fed the dog, because it was hungry. ✓
- I fed the dog, it was hungry.   ✗

Commas are used to mark off parts of a sentence that give extra information, but are not necessary for the sentence to make sense, for example:
- Amy , having eaten ten bananas , was feeling sick.
- Tom , the football captain , scored two goals.

The shaded phrases could be taken out and the sentences would still make sense.

Commas are used to list items, for example:
- He bought sugar, butter, eggs and flour.

Commas are also used to introduce speech, for example:
- 'I've had enough,' he cried, 'I'm going.'

Question Marks (?)

Question marks come at the end of questions. They are used in direct speech, but not in indirect (reported) speech, for example:
- 'Did you see Lizzie at the party?' asked Darren.   ✓
- Darren asked me if I'd seen Lizzie at the party?   ✗

Common Errors in Writing

Colons (:)

Colons are used before an explanation or example, for example:

- The marathon was a very long race: 26 miles!

Colons also appear before a list, for example:

- I got lots of presents: a book, a hat, loads of CDs.

The part before the colon must be a complete sentence, but the part after it does not need to be.

Semi-colons (;)

Semi-colons are used to show that two sentences are closely related, for example:

- The game may be cancelled; it depends on the weather.

The parts before and after the semi-colon must be complete sentences.

Apostrophes (')

Apostrophes are used to show omission or contraction (usually in speech or in informal writing). The apostrophe replaces the missing letter(s), for example:

- He shouldn't have eaten that. (Should not = shouldn't)
- You'll never understand. (You will = you'll)
- Mark's finished his work but Rachel's still doing hers. (Mark has = Mark's, Rachel is = Rachel's)

Apostrophes are also used to show possession (ownership). If the owner is singular, (or plural but does not end in 's', e.g. sheep, men, children), add an apostrophe and an 's' to the word that indicates the owner, for example:

- The cat's tail (i.e. the tail belonging to the cat)

- The boy's shoes (i.e. the shoes belonging to the boy)
- It was Lucy's idea (i.e. the idea belonging to Lucy)
- The children's books (i.e. the books belonging to the children)

If there is more than one owner and the word indicating the owners ends in 's', simply add an apostrophe at the end, for example:

- The cats' tails (i.e. the tails belonging to the cats)
- The boys' shoes (i.e. the shoes belonging to the boys)
- The girls' idea (i.e. the idea belonging to the girls)

Brackets ( )

Brackets are used to contain additional information that could be removed from the sentence without changing the meaning or flow, for example:

- Helsinki (the capital of Finland) is a beautiful city.

Confusing Words

Done / did, and seen / saw

These words are often used incorrectly.

- I did it
- I have done it
- I done it
- I saw it   ✓
- I have seen it   ✓
- I seen it   ✗

Could, would, should, ought to, might

These are modal verbs. They are never followed by 'of'. They are followed by 'have', for example:

- I could have won the race.   ✓
- I could of won the race.   ✗

Spelling

It is important that you spell and use words correctly. The following list contains words which are frequently misused. It will help you if you read through these words and learn the correct ways to spell them and use them.

Accept – to receive: 'I accept your gift with thanks'.
Except – without: 'all the boys went except John'.

Aloud – out loud: 'read your work aloud'.
Allowed – permitted: 'chewing is not allowed'.

Hear – to hear with your ears: 'I can hear music'.
Here – in this place: 'It's over here'.

Its – belonging to it: 'the cat licked its paws'.
It's – short for 'it is': 'it's a long way home'.

Lay / lie – The past tense of 'lie' is' lay': 'last night I lay on my bed for a while'.
In the present tense you 'lay a table' or, if you are a hen, 'lay an egg'.

No – opposite of 'yes': 'no, I didn't like it'.
New – opposite of old: 'it's a new bag'.
Know / knew – being aware of something: 'I didn't know Michael knew about it'.

Passed – a verb: 'I passed all my GCSEs'.
Past – a noun indicating a previous time: 'it's all in the past now'.
(Also used in phrases such as 'he went past' or 'they are past their best'.)

Practice – a noun: 'netball practice is cancelled'.
Practise – a verb: 'if you practise hard you might get into the team'.
(The same rule applies to advice / advise.)

Quite – fairly, a bit: 'the essay was quite good'.
Quiet – silent: 'I knew there was something wrong because the class was so quiet'.

Right – opposite of wrong: 'that is the right way'.
Write – what you do in an exam. Someone who writes is a writer: 'she writes well'.

There – in that place: 'I'll be there soon'.
(Also used in phrases such as 'there is', 'there are'.)
They're – 'they are' (the apostrophe shows that the 'a' is missing): 'they're not friends'.
Their – belonging to them: 'they left their bags on the bus'.

Too – excessively: 'we had too many sweets'.
Two – the number: 'the two bears'.
To – towards: 'he went to bed'.
(Also part of the infinitive of a verb, e.g. 'to do', 'to think'.)

Where – a place: 'where did you say it was?'.
We're – 'we are' (the apostrophe shows that the 'a' is missing): 'we're not sure'.
Wear – used with clothes, etc.: 'I will wear my gold earrings'.

Whether – if: 'I don't know whether to go or not'.
Weather – the sun, wind, rain, etc.: 'the weather was terrible'.

Whose – belonging to whom: 'whose coat is it?'.
Who's – 'who is' or 'who has': 'who's that boy? Who's dropped that coat?'

Your – belonging to you: 'It's your bag'.
You're – 'you are' (the apostrophe shows that the 'a' is missing): 'you're happy'.

Paragraphs

The assessor will be looking for evidence of paragraphs when marking your work. Paragraphs are used to organise pieces of writing. A paragraph is a set of sentences which have related ideas or subjects. Paragraphs are usually shown in one of two ways:

1 By leaving a line before starting a new paragraph:

> We believe that forcing students to wear an uncomfortable uniform is wrong.
>
> I realise that some people feel differently about uniform and believe its benefits outweigh its negative points.

2 By indenting the text when you start a new paragraph:

> We believe that forcing students to wear an uncomfortable uniform is wrong.
>   I realise that some people feel differently about uniform and believe its benefits outweigh its negative points.

When to Start a New Paragraph

Paragraphs are used to break up the text into groups of sentences. Using paragraphs means you do not end up with a solid block of text, and it allows you to present your writing in an organised way so that your ideas are easier to follow. A new paragraph is used when you have any of the following:

- **A change of time**, for example:

> During the summer holidays, Sarah decided to go to work at the animal sanctuary. The summer holidays were very long and Sarah loved being outdoors with the animals.
>
> When winter came with its dark nights, Sarah hated being outside.

- **A change of speaker**, for example:

> "Maybe we should have stayed," said Fern, "They might notice we're missing."
>
> "I think we should go home," said Rafferty.

- **A change of place or person**, for example:

> The hills surrounding the village are dominated by ten large wind turbines.
>
> The wooded valley, two miles from the village, is protected.

Helpful Hint

If, at the end of the exam, you realise you have forgotten to use paragraphs, mark where you would separate the paragraphs by inserting a slash where each paragraph break should be, e.g.

- We believe that forcing students to wear an uncomfortable uniform is wrong. **/** I realise that some people feel differently about uniform and believe it has many benefits.

You could also write 'NP' (new paragraph) in the margin, e.g.

- We believe that forcing students to wear an
NP uncomfortable uniform is wrong. **/** I realise that some people feel differently about uniform and believe it has many benefits.

Remember, this is not a replacement for paragraphs. Only use it if you forget.

Paragraphs

Beginning and Ending

Every piece of writing should have an opening paragraph and a closing (concluding) paragraph. The assessor/examiner wants to see that you have thought about the structure of your writing carefully so that the opening makes your intentions clear, and the conclusion summarises the main points.

Opening Paragraphs

A good opening paragraph in writing to persuade might flatter or compliment the reader to gain their interest. A good opening paragraph in writing to advise might offer a compliment or a sympathetic phrase to the reader to gain their trust and confidence.

Look at the example opposite of a good opening paragraph for writing to persuade.

In this example the writer states their view clearly, and recognises the opposing point. The writer uses the first and second person direct pronouns 'I' and 'you' to get the reader's attention and develop a personal tone.

Closing Paragraphs

A good conclusion to any piece of writing will summarise the main points you have made in your writing.

Look at the example opposite of a good concluding paragraph to the letter.

In this example the writer opens the final paragraph well with the use of 'In conclusion', and goes on to summarise the main points of the letter, including the opposing viewpoint. The writer rounds the letter off well by suggesting that she expects a response.

An Opening Paragraph

96 Oak Close,
Southampton.

Daily News,
1 Main Street,
Southampton

10th March 2010

Dear Sir/Madam

I am writing to you to voice my opposition to the building of a supermarket on the recreation ground in the village. Whilst I am strongly against this proposal I do recognise that there are some equally important issues about the lack of a supermarket in the village that need addressing.

cont...

A Concluding Paragraph

In conclusion, I feel I have shown that the recreation ground is vital to the village in many ways and, whilst the problems of the elderly and access to supermarkets do need addressing, I feel that this cannot be at the expense of village life. I hope you take my proposals on board and I look forward to hearing from you in the future.

Yours faithfully

D Jeffries

Mrs D Jeffries

Connectives

To obtain the higher grades you need to use a variety of sentence structures in your writing, both in the exam and in your controlled assessment tasks.

Connectives (connectors) are used to extend your sentences and show that you can create complex sentences. Connectives are words and phrases that link paragraphs, sentences or parts of sentences (clauses), for example, 'although', 'because', 'but'.

Simple, Compound and Complex Sentences

A **simple sentence** is the most basic type of sentence structure. For example:

- 'The man walked towards me.'

A **compound sentence** consists of two clauses, joined together by a connective. For example:

- 'The man walked towards me **and** I could see that he meant harm.'

A **complex sentence** contains one main clause (or independent clause) and at least one subordinate clause (or dependent clause). For example:

- Although I am extremely upset with John (**subordinate clause**), I want to go to the club with him because Jack will be there! (**main clause**)

Connectives allow the sentence and the ideas in it to be extended. They add value to all types of writing.

Connectives in Writing to Persuade

Connectives can be particularly useful when you are writing to persuade. They can be used very effectively to open or close a point of view. They also enable you to start your sentences in a variety of ways, which is a good way to boost your grade. For example:

- '**Firstly**, I would like to note that…'
- '**Clearly**, we are living in dangerous times…'
- 'In **conclusion**, I feel that…'

Connectives can be used:

- **At the beginning of a sentence**, for example:
  - '**Naturally**, some people will say that we are free to choose our own future…'
- **In the middle of a sentence**, for example:
  - 'Caving in winter is dangerous **because** the caves can fill quickly with water'.
- **To connect paragraphs** and give cohesion to your writing, for example:
  - 'We think that forcing students to wear uniform is wrong.
  Obviously I know that some people feel differently…'.

Connectives in Writing to Inform / Instruct

Connectives can be useful in writing to inform or instruct because they allow you to state the issue and then connect it naturally to the subject you are trying to inform or instruct the audience about. For example:

- 'This can be a problem. **Therefore**, I felt it would help you to…'
- 'This may be quite stressful. **So** I thought you might like to…'
- 'I don't mean to bother you, **but**…'

Here is a list of some of the more commonly used connectives. It may help you to learn some of these so that you can use them effectively in your writing.

- First of all
- Most importantly
- In addition
- Finally
- Nevertheless
- Even so
- Therefore
- For example
- However
- Although
- Equally
- Despite
- Consequently

Preparation Task

Using the connectives on this page, write a letter to your school newspaper, summarising your argument about an issue you feel strongly about (e.g. the need for year 11 students to be treated differently to the rest of the school).

Cohesion and Fluency

Cohesion

Cohesion is the way that you structure your piece of writing so that it all makes sense and fits together in a logical and flowing (cohesive) way.

If you do not have cohesion in your writing, it can seem disjointed and will not flow well.

Cohesion can be achieved through linking your paragraphs, as seen on page 80. The speech about smoking on page 51 is a cohesive text.

Cohesion can be achieved by doing the following:

- Starting paragraphs in a similar way, for example:
    - *'The first point that I am going to make is…'*
      'The second reason this is not allowed is…'
      'The third reason for this is…'
- Referring back to previous topics or paragraphs, for example:
    - *'As stated earlier…'*
      'As we saw previously…'
      'Therefore, as we have seen,…'
- Linking the last line of the previous paragraph with the first line of the next one, for example:
    - *'For this reason, tigers will be extinct within the next 20 years.*
      So, what can be done to help these beautiful creatures?'

Fluency

When we say that a speaker is fluent in a language it means that they can use the language well – almost as well as a native speaker. But even though a person may be fluent in a language, they may not be fluent in the language use.

Fluency Tips

Fluency in speech can be helped through practice. Practice makes perfect – if you are delivering a speech, practise it first.

Fluency in writing comes through using the skills covered in this chapter. Your writing has to flow and follow a logical structure.

Helpful Hint

If you have cohesion, fluency will follow. Your work must be structured to make the sequence of events and development of ideas clear and coherent to the audience.

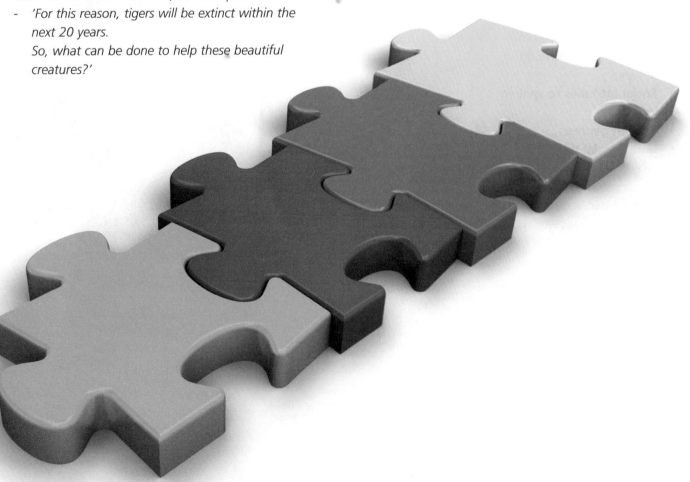

Spoken Language Study

Unit 3, Part C: Spoken Language Study

This section refers to Unit 3, Part C of the English Language course. It applies to students studying the English Language course only.

However, the skills outlined in this chapter will be really useful for preparation for Unit 2 of both the English Language course *and* the English course, Speaking and Listening.

Both courses require you to respond to different texts and the following pages will enhance your ability to do this.

Spoken Language Study

Controlled Assessment

For the Spoken Language Study part of the English Language course, you must complete one task:
- It should be 800–1000 words in length.
- It can be delivered as an oral presentation.
- You may work in pairs or groups to prepare for the assessment, but the final task will need to be written up or presented individually.

You only have to do one of the controlled assignments for spoken language. You will choose one of the following three topics:
- **Social attitudes to spoken language.**
- **Spoken genres.**
- **Multi-modal talk.**

Choose the one that you are most interested in.

If you think that you are better at presentation than writing, choose to deliver your work this way as this is allowed in this part of the controlled assessment.

What is the Assessor Looking For?

For this part of the English Language course, the assessor wants to see that you can:
- Apply the terms that are used when analysing spoken language.
- Respond to a spoken text in the same analytical way in which you would respond to a written text.
- Explain and evaluate how and why certain language features are used.

Social Attitudes to Spoken Language

Social attitudes were touched on briefly in the Standard English and non-standard variations of English section (pages 40–41). Because people speak differently – due to accents and dialects – stereotypes and attitudes towards certain ways of speaking have developed.

Here is a list of terms and explanations that are important for you to consider:

- **Idiolect** – each of us has our own form of language. The language that each individual uses is unique. It is individual to each person, like a fingerprint.
- **Accent** – each of us has our own sound when we pronounce words. For example, Ant and Dec have a 'Geordie' accent that makes them sound friendly and approachable.
- **Dialect** – the words that we use may differ, for example, 'chuddy' is used to mean chewing gum in some parts of the country.
- **We use words from our background, upbringing and culture**. If a child hears their parents swearing all the time, they too might swear a lot as they would be used to hearing the words and might think that they are acceptable.
- **We use words that reflect our age** – a ten-year-old who watches a lot of American television might start using the word 'dude' to mean 'friend', but their grandmother would be unlikely to use it!

- **We use words that reflect our education** – for example, it has been proven that people who work in university environments have very developed vocabularies because they deal with the written word a lot of the time, and are surrounded by highly educated people. We use words that are specific to our job or occupation.

Past Attitudes to Language

In the past, there were a lot of ideas about spoken language that are not always upheld today. Here are some of them:

- People who use Standard English and Received Pronunciation must be posh and have a lot of money.
- Only well-educated people use 'proper English'.
- To be on television, people have to 'speak properly' and not have a regional accent.
- Slang words and colloquial words are only used by young people and people who are not well-educated.

Do you agree or disagree with these statements?

Preparation Task

When you are watching television, look out for people using words that are specific to the job that they are doing, which are not part of everyday language. *The Bill* and *Casualty* are good examples.

'dude!'

Social Attitudes to Spoken Language

Spoken Language Versus Written Language

Spoken English used to be seen as an inferior form of English to the written language.

Spoken language often has regional accents and is spontaneous – it just spills out, so it can sometimes come out in the wrong way. I'm sure you can think of a time when you thought, 'Why did I say that?'.

Written language can be drafted and corrected. It does not have an accent (although writers can write to depict an accent) and Standard English is usually used. In many forms of writing, anything other than Standard English would not be acceptable. For example, you would not apply for the job of your dreams in 'e-mail' or 'text' speak, would you?

Despite the fact that society has changed a lot in recent years, some people are still not happy about the 'dilution of the English language'.

Nowadays, informal language is used a lot more in formal situations. For example, the BBC news used to be upheld as the 'correct' way to use language. No informal words, colloquial terms or slang would be used. It would be delivered using Standard English, in Received Pronunciation. While today this is often still the case, regional accents are now frequently used and colloquial words may also be used. For example, a weather reporter might report in the weather forecast that it is going to 'chuck it down' (slang). This would have got a lot of complaints 20 years ago, but today, most people would not even notice.

Nowadays, regional accents can be heard on many television programmes – by children's television hosts, football commentators, chat show hosts, etc. Look out for the variety of accents that now exist on television.

In the past, regional accents were seen to show that people were not well educated or that they came from the lower classes or did not have much money. This cannot be said today. For example, Charlotte Church is a very rich woman but she still has a regional accent!

Even today, some people still believe that it is 'better' to use Standard English and try to have an accent that resembles Received Pronunciation. For example, if you were going for a job interview, or addressing an audience of people that you did not know, you would probably put on your 'best accent' and avoid using slang words. However, when you are with your friends you might try to have a strong regional accent and use non-standard English words to try to be part of the gang.

Many young people try to copy the 'street language' found in rap music to try to sound cool and streetwise. Speaking like Dizzee Rascal might be fine with your friends, but it would not go down well in a job interview and would not get you a good grade in your English exam!

Helpful Hint

Remember, the way that you write and the way that you speak are different. Go back to form, language, audience and purpose. You must use the appropriate language for the situation.

When you are responding to texts written in the past it is worth remembering that writers in the past did use accents and dialects to show a character's social class and level of education.

Varieties of Spoken Language

Spoken language can cover a wide variety of language. It can be divided into **informal language** (and situations) and **formal language** (and situations).

Informal Spoken Language

Features of informal spoken language include:
- Slang.
- Colloquial language.
- Accent.
- Dialectal words.
- Informal register.

Informal spoken language is used:
- When you are speaking to your friends.
- When you are speaking on the phone to somebody you know.
- When you are telling a joke.
- In play scripts for teenagers.
- In film scripts that reflect real characters in informal situations.
- In continuous drama/soap scripts.
- In interviews with celebrities on the radio or television.
- In documentaries featuring informal situations or characters in informal situations.

Formal Spoken Language

Features of formal spoken English include:
- Standard English.
- Formal tone and register.
- Received Pronunciation.

Formal spoken language is used:
- In television broadcasts on a serious topic.
- In school assemblies.
- In interviews with politicians.
- In job interviews.
- When teachers talk in class.
- When you are giving a talk or presentation to a large audience of people on a serious subject.
- When you are speaking to people who you do not know very well and are trying to impress!
- When you are giving a public talk – where you are talking to an audience/the general public.

Code Switching

Everybody has the ability to 'code-switch', i.e. to change their language depending on their audience.

You will not use the same language when talking to your parents as you will when talking to your friends.

Teachers code-switch all the time. If you could record them in the staff room talking to their colleagues, then again delivering a lesson to a Year 7 class, they would probably sound very different and use different words.

Other Types of Spoken Language

The following are some other variations to consider:
- **Spontaneous spoken language** – you speak without even thinking about it, for example, when you respond in conversations with your friends or on the phone.
- **Considered spoken language** – if you were in an interview, you would stop and think before answering the question and may put on your 'best accent'.
- **Language that is written to be spoken** – for example, a speech to the class. You would write it first and then speak the words. The language has been drafted and you might use Standard English to speak it, if the audience requires this form of language.
- **Language that is written to sound like real spoken language** – for example, the scripts written for soap opera characters, play scripts or film scripts.

These forms of spoken language are different to each other.

Spontaneous Spoken Language

Features of Spontaneous Language

Spontaneous spoken language has a number of features:

Accent – you can hear an accent and perhaps tell where the speaker comes from.

Dialect – people use words that they know might not be Standard English when they speak, but their social groups use them, so they do too.

Turn-taking – when people speak, they take it in turns to speak. This is polite conversation. However, sometimes, people cannot help themselves and they interrupt the person who is speaking.

Holding the floor – people take over and start talking. If they do not stop, it is called 'holding the floor'.

Pausing – people often pause when they speak. When they are considering what to say next or lose their train of thought halfway through the conversation, they pause. Writers often use '...' to show that a person has paused; sometimes the length of the pause is put in brackets for a film or TV script, e.g. (2 mins).

Back-tracking and repetition – sometimes people go back in a conversation to where they were before. When you write things down it is obvious if you repeat yourself. But when people speak, they are not always aware that they have done it. Sometimes, people repeat things if they do not know how to move on or have forgotten what they were going to say.

Tone – when you speak, you use the right tone of voice for what you are saying. If you were telling your friend that your dog had died, you would sound sad. If you were telling them that your dad had won the lottery, you would sound delighted!

Structure – people often do not use full sentences when they speak. People do not need to talk in full sentences to be understood. In spontaneous speech, people respond to what is said before, and refer back to what has been said without actually directly referring to it. For example:
- Jack: Did you watch EastEnders last night?
  Jessica: Good, wasn't it
  Jack: Hate that Phil though, don't you?
  Jessica: Yeah

Both times Jessica speaks, and the second time Jack speaks, they rely on what was said before so that what they say make sense.

Spontaneous Spoken Language

Pace Sometimes people speak quickly; other times they speak slowly. It depends on the situation and who they are speaking to.

Pitch – People sound high-pitched when they are excited, and they have a low pitch when they are sad.

Intonation – People's voices vary as they speak. For example, if you read the following sentences aloud, your voice should go up and down:
-   'Say this out loud as if you really mean it.'
-   'I am the most adorable, intelligent and superb creature.'

When people ask questions and say exclamatory sentences, their voices go up at the end. For example, read the following sentences aloud:
-   'What do you mean?'
-   'I don't believe it!'

Fillers – when you have a moment where you cannot think of what to say, you fill the gap with 'fillers'. Fillers include:
-   'erm...'
-   'er...'
-   'mmm...'

Social Attitudes to Spoken Language – Example Assessment Tasks

Let us look at the type of task that you could be set based around the topic of social attitudes to spoken language.

Any task in this part of the course will require you to use the terms that describe features of spontaneous spoken language.

Q Examine your own personal language use. What are the key features of the language that you use?

Q Investigate the language used by a certain type of song lyrics. Why do some adults complain about this type of language?

For the first task above, you would need to be able to identify the language features that you use yourself, and comment upon them.

For the second task above, you would need to choose a type of music to study the lyrics from – probably rap lyrics or hip hop lyrics would give you most to discuss.

You need to know about the use of Standard English and non-standard variations to do the tasks well. You must consider social attitudes to language – you might not agree with them but you must acknowledge that you know about them.

Refer back to the Speaking and Listening section on pages 39–51 to help you do this well.

Helpful Hint

You can do this controlled assessment task as a written piece or as a presentation. Do it in the form that you think you are best at.

It is worth 10% of your final marks.

Practice Question

Write a response to the task:

Q Examine your own personal language use. What are the key features of the language that you use?

Planned Speech

Written, or planned, speech can try to reflect spoken language on occasions. For example, the script writers of films, television dramas, novels, plays and dramatic monologues want their characters to sound as realistic as possible, so that they are believable characters. Therefore, this means they will have to use the features of spontaneous speech when they write.

Writers will give characters certain accents to reflect their personalities or ways of life. They will have characters using regional dialects to make them realistic and believable. They will have to highlight these features for the performance of the speech.

Written Features to Reflect Spontaneous Speech

The following are features that writers use to reflect spontaneous speech in their scripts.

Pauses

Writers often use '…' to show that a person has paused, or they give the length of the pause in brackets for a film or television script, e.g. (10 secs).

You might put a pause into a speech that you were going to deliver if you wanted to make a dramatic point or to give your audience time to consider what you had just said. For example:
- 'I think we should all care about the plight of these wonderful creatures… don't you?' (pause again and then look up at the audience).

Brackets

In play scripts, film scripts, drama scripts and monologues, brackets are used to hold information for the characters/actors, directors and producers.

When you read a script as a mere reader, you need to make sure that you take these brackets into account, otherwise you could miss vital information about the characters' feelings or behaviour. For example:
- Adnan: (suspiciously) Are you really going to leave that to me?
- Jade: I know that we haven't always got along (pacing across the room repeatedly)

The brackets give us additional information about the characters – how they are thinking and feeling and how the lines should be spoken.

Abbreviations / Contractions

Abbreviations or contractions such as 'haven't' ('have not') and 'couldn't' ('could not') are a feature of informal language. When we speak, we tend to use them more than the full form.

Interruptions

If you see this sign // in a script, it means that there is overlap with the characters talking. It can indicate an interruption. Stronger characters tend to interrupt weaker ones, both in scripts and in real life. However, sometimes we cannot help ourselves and we interrupt the person who is speaking.

Bold font or italics

A bold font or italic font is used to indicate that a word needs to be stressed. For example:
- 'You boy, **you**, the one at the back!'

Adjectives, adverbs and verbs

In novels, writers use adjectives, adverbs and interesting verbs to show how the words are spoken by the characters, to reflect what they are thinking and feeling. For example:
- 'Jamila was **upset** as she said…' (Adjective)
- '**Distractedly**, Jevan whispered…' (Adverb)
- 'Simone **screamed**, 'I don't believe you…' ' (Verb)

Helpful Hint

Writers use the features of spontaneous speech in their writing to make the language of the characters seem realistic.

Remember, there are techniques to writing good speeches that are more formal (see pages 49–51).

Differences in Speech and Writing

Sometimes, the differences between speech and writing are not that obvious. Some speech is written down first, so in this case, writing becomes speech on its delivery!

However, we have also seen that there are some differences between the two. The table illustrates this in its simplest form.

Speech	Writing
Although in the past, many could not write, everyone could speak. But those who used standard English and Received Pronunciation were given the same respect as those who could write. They were considered to be wealthy and educated.	In the past the literate were usually those who had the wealth and power in society, so being able to write had respect/prestige.
It is often spontaneous and not planned.	It is planned and crafted by the writer.
It can be formal or informal depending on the form, language, audience and purpose (FLAP).	It can be formal or informal depending on the form, language, audience and purpose (FLAP).
Pauses are not planned – we use them whilst we are thinking about what to say next.	Pauses are planned and indicated by writing techniques such as … or (5 secs).
Repetition is used unintentionally in spontaneous speech, and used for effect in planned speeches (see speech on page 67).	Repetition is used by writers to emphasise or stress certain points or words.
Speech does not use Standard English grammar that you would find in writing – words can be missed out without affecting the meaning, for example: - *Going to the park?*	Standard English grammar is used in almost all types of writing, for example: - *Are you going to the park?*

Spoken Genres

There are many different spoken genres, including:

- Scripts.
- Transcriptions of real conversations.
- Speeches for a public audience.
- Political speeches.
- Speeches in parliament.
- School assemblies.
- Telephone conversations.

Each will have features that you are expected to know.

You have to be able to show that you can:

- Adapt your own speech according to the situation.
- Recognise Standard English and its use.
- Explain and evaluate how you and others use and adapt language for specific purposes.

Example Assessment Tasks Based Around Spoken Genres

Here are two examples of the type of controlled assessment task you could get in this part of the course:

Q **How does the language used in your favourite continuous drama (soap opera) try to represent real speech?**

Q **Investigate the language use of a particular job.**

Transcribing Speech

How to Transcribe a Text

This page gives an example of the sort of spoken text that you might have to analyse in the spoken language assessment task. The things that you will need to be able to spot and write about (i.e. explore/investigate) are also listed.

To be able to analyse spontaneous speech you will need to record it first. When you have recorded it you will need to **transcribe** it (i.e. set it out on paper) in the following way:

1 Write the speaker's name at the side, as in a play script. Set it out as a play script would look. You do not need to use speech marks as it is all speech. You may have been taught that you do not need to use punctuation either.

2 Use empty square brackets to show words that you cannot hear or understand.

3 Use brackets or ... to show pauses.

4 Make sure you show all fillers / hesitations such as 'uh', 'um', 'er'.

5 If body language or non-verbal communication is important, indicate it in normal or square brackets, for example, (everyone laughs), [very rapid speech].

6 Loud noise or shouting can be shown by capital letters or bold and larger font.

7 Exclamations can be marked with exclamation marks, '!'.

8 Stressed words or words that you want to emphasise can be shown by using italics.

9 Overlapping speech – square brackets show where the overlapping speech begins. For example:
- *Jan:* *Tell us about yourself.*
  [
  Andy: *Let me tell you about myself.*

10 Accent and dialect can be hard to show, especially non-standard English accents. For example, 'I can't do it', in a Jamaican accent might look like this:
- *I cay-ant do it.*

You can write accents as they might sound, or look like they would sound. Make sure that you show it is not-standard if you need to show accent.

It is acceptable to write the words in full when an accent is used, but make sure you comment on the accent, as below:
- *This example transcript is spoken in a Leeds accent.*

Then you can treat the transcript like any other text and apply the same techniques to explore/investigate it.

Example Transcript

This is what part of a transcript might look like:

> Adil: We goin' t' park tonight?
>
> Jake: Er, no ... I'm goin' to the pics wi' Claire
>   [
> Adil: Ahh... YOU SAID YOU WOULD!
>
> Jake: NO NEED TO SHOUT!
>
> Adil: (laughing) Very funny

Helpful Hint

Remember to transcribe the speech accurately – as it sounds, not as it *should* or *could* sound.

Assessment Task Terms

The following are some words and phrases that you might encounter in the assessment tasks. Here is a quick guide as to what the assessor wants you to do:

- **Investigate** – transcribe and write about.
- **Reflect** – write about and give examples.
- **How does…** – look at the text and write about it, using the technical terms.
- **What devices…** – apply the language analysis terms that you know to the text.

Analysing a Spoken Text

As with all texts, when you are analysing a spoken text, remember to comment on the following:

- **Form / genre** – e.g. a written speech, a play script, a transcript
- **Language** – formal, informal, use of accent, etc.
- **Audience** – social group or types of people
- **Purpose** – e.g. to persuade, to interact with friends, to entertain.

Remember to use the PEE technique in your analysis, e.g.

P Point – *The speaker uses repetition.*

E Evidence – *'I don't, I don't really know'*

E Explanation – *This shows that they are unsure about what they are saying and it suggests that they are not very confident in the situation.*

Example Exploration of a Text

Read the following spoken text. What features of spontaneous speech can you see in it?

Adil: We goin' t' park tonight?

Jake: Er, no … I'm goin' to the pics wi' Claire
          [

Adil: Ahh… YOU SAID YOU WOULD! Knew you'd let me down… *again.*

Jake: NO NEED TO SHOUT!

Adil: (laughing) Very funny

Jake: You still goin' wi' Sarah?

Adil: Might be (sniggering and looking down at the ground)

The following are some points you might comment on:

- The grammatical word 'Are' is left out – a feature of informal language and spontaneous speech.
- The filler 'er' shows a reluctance to answer.
- … pause – Jake pauses because he is not giving the answer that he knows his friend wants to hear. This suggests that he had said he *would* go and that he knows his friend will be disappointed.
- Overlap – Adil knows that his friend is going to say no, even before he says it and this is shown in the way he interrupts the answer. This suggests that they are good friends who know each other well.
- Capital letters show that he has shouted the words, which suggests that Adil is a bit angry with his friend.
- 'Again' – this word in italics shows that Adil stressed it, suggesting that this has happened before.
- Jake then makes light of the situation with the joke, 'NO NEED TO SHOUT!'. The capitals show that he is shouting too, and it had the effect that he wants. He makes his friend laugh.
- Jake then changes the subject and asks about Sarah. He does not use a full sentence here; he uses a phrase: 'You still goin' wi' Sarah?'. Again grammatical words are left out, as is typical of speech. Also, the sentence could make us ask, 'Going where?' But we know that this is a colloquial phrase used by teenagers to mean going out with someone.
- Finally, Adil is looking down at the ground when he gives his reply. This suggests that he is embarrassed or shy. His body language implies this.

Multi-modal Language

What is Multi-modal Language?

A multi-modal language is one that involves different types of communication.

Multi-modal talk is a method of communication using different types of talk. It involves different styles. A mode is a style.

Examples of multi-modal communication include:
- On-line chat rooms.
- Using the Internet to communicate with others – war games, dating sites, Facebook, Bebo, Twitter, etc.
- Texting.
- Using a BlackBerry® to send messages.
- Mobile phone communications.
- Message boards – used to carry on a conversation, request information and give messages.

You might be writing (texting) but using more of a spoken type of language. Indeed, texting has now got its own language!

An on-line chat room is the perfect example of multi-modality. You are 'chatting', which suggests talking, but in fact you are writing. However, the writing will use language that is more like spoken language than written language.

When you are analysing any of these forms of multi-modal communication, you have to use all the range of language analysis tools that you have, as these forms of language use elements from all types of texts and communications.

But, the form of language mostly used in multi-modal communications or exchanges will reflect the spoken word.

Internet Language

Chat, e-mail, web, and chat room slang and acronyms have become well used. Acronyms are abbreviations that use the initial letters of the words that they represent. Some examples are shown in the table.

Acronym	Meaning
AAK	Alive And Kicking
AAR	At Any Rate
AAS	Alive And Smiling
ADN	Any Day Now
AFAIK	As Far As I Know
AFK	Away From the Keyboard
AFN	That's All For Now
AOTA	All Of The Above
a/s/l or asl	Age/Sex/Location – (used to ask a chatter their personal information)
AV	Avatar – graphical representation (a picture) often used in chat rooms to depict a person who is in the room and chatting.
b4	Before
BAK	Back At Keyboard ('I'm back')
BBL	Be Back Later
BBS	Be Back Soon
BCNU	I'll Be Seeing You
b/f	Boyfriend (also shown as bf, B/F, or BF)
BFN	Bye For Now
boot	To get kicked out of a chat room, or to have to restart the computer because you couldn't talk in the chat room anymore.
BR	Best Regards
BRB	Be Right Back

Helpful Hint

Standard English is still the language of the exams. So, whilst you might be a multi-modal expert, remember to use Standard English when it is required.

Everyday Language

The 'Internet' or 'text' language discussed on the previous page has only evolved since the invention of the machines on which we do this type of communication.

Teenagers tend to be fluent in this type of language, whereas your parents might not know what many of the acronyms mean, and they probably do not use them in their own text messages.

Language changes all the time. You only have to look at a Shakespeare play compared to the language used today to see this in action.

Some people think that the 'Internet' or 'text' type of language is 'inferior' to Standard English. It is definitely a non-standard variation of English, but if you are a teenager it is the language of everyday life.

Different Types of Everyday Language

Think about the different forms of language that you might use in a typical day. For example:
- Getting up and speaking to your parents.
- Shouting at your little brother.
- Texting your friend about meeting later.
- Answering questions in your history class.
- Talking about a science experiment.
- Going out at break and chatting with your friends.
- Phoning your mum to ask her to pick you up.

- Calling to your friends whilst playing a sport.
- Going on-line and joining a chat room.
- E-mailing your friend.
- Writing up an English essay about a novel.
- Texting your boyfriend/girlfriend to say goodnight.

These are only a fraction of the different ways that you will use language during a typical day. Notice how each one is different, and how you will use different language in each situation.

Without thinking about it, you will consider FLAP whenever you communicate:
- **Form/genre** – e.g. are you texting?
- **Language** – e.g. can you be formal or informal?
- **Audience** – e.g. do not send the text that you send to your girlfriend or boyfriend to your mum or dad!
- **Purpose** – e.g. are you communicating to be sociable, or are you trying to tell someone something?

Without realising it, you are a real language expert. It could be said that you are more of an expert than your parents or grandparents because you are 'up-to-date'!

Helpful Hint

It is crucial that you use the right language in the right situation.

Spoken Language Study – Example

Example Assessment Task Based on Multi-modal Talk

Here is an example of the type of controlled assessment task you could get in this part of the course:

> **Q** **How does the way that you 'chat' in an on-line chat room differ to the way that you chat with your friends?**
> **Investigate 8 similarities and differences, giving examples of each.**

You are aiming to write approximately 800–1000 words (i.e. about 3 sides of script). This task is worth 10% of your final mark.

Example Response Template

Here is an example of how you could approach the task.

1. **Get your data.**
   Print a chat response off the Internet. Make sure you get permission to do so from the person you are chatting to. Then, record a conversation between your friends, or make notes during a conversation.
2. **Transcribe the conversation.**
   See page 90 for tips on how to transcribe speech.
3. **Highlight interesting features of each of the scripts.**
4. **Apply the terms that you have learned.**
   But do not forget the other terms that you have learned for studying language, as many of them may be applicable (relevant).

Example Response

Introduction

The following is an example of an introduction to the task.

During the course of the study, I am going to examine ways in which chat room 'chat' resembles everyday chat among a group of friends. I am going to focus on eight main features.

Main Body of the Assessment

Write a paragraph about each of the eight features – eight paragraphs. Remember to use the PEE technique.

An example paragraph in the study might read:

One common feature between chat room chat and normal conversation is the informality of the language. When we chat with people that we know we tend to use informal language. For example, 'We off down the

chippy?', instead of, 'Are we going to the fish and chip shop?', which would be the Standard English way to express this. We miss out grammatical words as they are not necessary in chat because the meaning is still clear. Also, we do not have to refer to the specific time because we are referring to the present time.

Conclusion

Sum up what you have found out and the conclusion that you have reached.

Here is an example conclusion:

Therefore, as we can see from the study, chat room exchanges and informal chatting with friends share many common features. This backs up the theory that the divisions between spoken language and written language are being broken down by the 'new' forms of conversation.

Spoken Language Summary

Here is a list of the terms that will be useful for you in any form of assessment with regard to spoken language. It might be in analysis of live language, or it might be the speech of characters in the texts that you are studying, or even in the Unit 1 examination.

This list should not be thought of in isolation – all the language terms throughout this revision guide might be useful.

Terms to Apply to a Spoken Language Summary

Dialect: the words and grammar that speakers use. Regional dialects differ from the Standard English dialect. Each dialect has its own special words and ways of using grammar.

Received Pronunciation: the accent used by many national newsreaders. This accent is seen as prestigious (impressive) and used to be associated with social groups that were well-educated and wealthy.

Standard English: the conventional or 'correct' use of words and grammar in the English language.

Tone: the tone of voice that is used to express the utterance. The tone of voice that someone uses can tell us how they are feeling.

Pauses: shown by … or brackets, e.g. (2 secs). They can show that someone is unsure of what to say next, but they are dependent on context.

Fillers: sounds used to fill pauses, e.g. 'erm', 'er'. These

can reveal that a character is lying or has forgotten what to say. These are dependent on context.

False starts / hesitations: e.g. 'I… I… I…'. It appears that the speaker is about to speak but then does not.

Repetition: repeating words or phrases. This can be in order to stress something or because the speaker is not sure what to say next.

Lack of grammatical words: e.g. lack of modal verbs – 'shall', 'could', etc. This is because speech does not require them to help with meaning or time and place.

Idiolect: each individual has their own language. The language that each person uses is unique.

Formal language: language register associated with formal situations.

Informal language: language register associated with informal situations.

Preparation Task

Complete this list by giving an example for each of the terms. Using your own examples will help you to understand and remember the terms.

Then, using the whole of the guide, find all the terms that you think could be applied to language study and continue this list. This is excellent revision for the whole course.

Index

A

Abbreviations 88
Accent 11, 41, 58, 83, 86
Adapting language 42
Adjectives 11, 20, 58
Adverbs 11, 20, 58
Alliteration 10, 11, 58
Analysing persuasive features 25
Analysing spoken text 91
Apostrophes 76
Articles 74
Assonance 11
Attitudes to language 83
Audience 8, 9, 14–15, 29, 31

B

Back-tracking 86
Bias 20
Body language 45
Brackets 76, 88

C

Camera shots 64
Characterisation and voice 55
Characters 52, 62
Code switching 85
Cohesion 81
Colons 76
Colour 22
Commas 75
Communication 42
Comparative devices 32
Connectives 80
Context 43
Contractions 88
Contrast 11, 58, 49
Creative non-fiction texts 71–73
Creative texts 52

D

Delivering a speech 50
Descriptive writing 69
Dialect 11, 41, 58, 83, 86, 95
Differences in speech and writing 89
Discussing and listening 39, 47

E

Emotive language 10, 20, 49
Everyday language 93
Exaggeration 10, 21

Exam terms 17
Exclamations 11, 58
Exclamatory sentences 21

F

Facial expressions 44
Fact 24
Factors affecting language 41
False starts 95
Fillers 86, 95
Film script 66
FLAP 8, 27
Fluency 81
Form 8, 9, 28, 56
Formal spoken language 85
Functional skills 5

G

Genre 8, 28, 52, 56

H

Headlines 22
Humour 11, 58
Hyperbole 10, 21

I

Idiolect 83, 95
Imagery 12, 58
Images 22
Informal spoken language 85
Informative writing 19
Instructive writing 19
Internet language 92
Interruptions 88
Intonation 86
Irony 12, 58

J

Juxtaposition 12, 21, 58

L

Language 8, 9, 30
Language change 42
Layout 22
Leaflets 34
Letters 32, 33

M

Media 63–64
Media texts 7
Metaphors 12, 58
Mood 10
Moving images 63–64
Multi-modal language 92

N

Narrative voice 10
Negative diction 20
Non-fiction text example 16
Non-fiction texts 7
Non-standard variations of English 41
Non-verbal communication 44

O

Onomatopoeia 12, 59
Opinion 24

P

Pace 86
Paragraphs 78
Parallelism 49
Pauses 88, 95
Pausing 86
PEE technique 23, 59
Personal pronouns 10, 20, 49
Personification 12, 59
Persuasive features 24
Persuasive speeches 50
Persuasive writing 20, 23
Pitch 86
Planned speech 88
Planning your writing 36
Play script 68
Poetry 69
Positive diction 20
Presentation 8, 9, 28
Presentational devices 22, 34
Presenting 39, 46
Producing creative texts 70
Producing non-fiction texts 27
Puns 12
Purpose 8, 9, 29

Q

Question marks 75
Questions 59

R

Received Pronunciation 12, 40, 59, 95
Relationships 52
Repetition 10, 13, 21, 32, 49, 59, 95
Responding to creative texts 60
Rhetorical questions 10, 13, 32, 49, 59
Rhyme 13

Rhythm 13
Role play 39, 48

S

Sarcasm 12, 58
Semi-colons 76
Sensational language 10
Sentences 80
Settings 52
Similes 13, 59
Slang 59
Social context 43
Sound effects 64
Speeches 49, 67
Spelling 77
Spoken genres 89
Spoken language 84
Spontaneous spoken language 85, 86
Standard English 13, 40, 59, 95
Style 9, 30, 52
Style features 10
Superlatives 13, 21
Symbolism 13

T

Themes 52
Themes and ideas 54
Tone 9, 10, 13, 20, 59, 86, 95
Transcribing speech 90
Turn-taking 86
Types of creative texts 66–69
Types of writing 18

U

Use of three 10, 32, 49

V

Verbal context 43

W

Writing tips 37
Writing to advise 35
Writing to inform 33
Writing to persuade 32
Written language 84